MW00635421

# Practical Security Training

## Patrick Kane, CPP

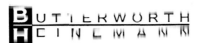

BUTTERWORTH
HEINEMANN

Boston  Oxford  Auckland  Johannesburg  Melbourne  New Delhi

Recognizing the importance of preserving what has been written, Butterworth–
Heinemann prints its books on acid-free paper whenever possible.

 Butterworth–Heinemann supports the efforts of American Forests and
the Global ReLeaf program in its campaign for the betterment of trees,
forests, and our environment.

Library of Congress Cataloging-in-Publication Data

Kane, Patrick, 1966–
    Practical security training / by Patrick Kane.
        p.    cm.
    Includes bibliographical references.
    ISBN 0-7506-7159-9 (pbk. : alk. paper)
    1. Police, Private—In-service training Handbooks, manuals, etc.   2. Private
security services Handbooks, manuals, etc.   I.  Title.
HV8290.K37     1999
363.28'9'0683—dc21                                                    99-26836
                                                                          CIP

British Library Cataloguing-in-Publication Data
A catalogue record for this book is available from the British Library.

The publisher offers special discounts on bulk orders of this book.
For information, please contact:
Manager of Special Sales
Butterworth–Heinemann
225 Wildwood Avenue
Woburn, MA 01801-2041
Tel: 781-904-2500
Fax: 781-904-2620

For information on all Butterworth–Heinemann publications available,
contact our World Wide Web home page at: http://www.bh.com

Printed in the United States of America

Transferred to Digital Printing 2007

This book is dedicated to the memory of my parents, Elizabeth and Bill Kane.

# Contents

# Contents

# Preface and Acknowledgements

Security personnel are increasingly being given more responsibility and facing more sophisticated threats than ever before. Training and professional development must keep pace with these changes if the security department is to continue to effectively protect the organization. *Practical Security Training* was written to assist security managers and trainers in developing more effective and realistic training programs. Better training will lead to better quality security personnel and therefore a safer, more secure workplace. Only by undertaking realistic, performance-based training will security personnel be able to meet the challenges of the future. Practical training techniques provide the best tool for realistically preparing the security force to deal effectively with a wide range of situations.

*Practical Security Training* borrows many of its methods and techniques from military training. The military is an institution that is concerned with preparedness, continuous training, and threat realization. These are all valid concerns for the security practitioner. Military units also deal with multiple commitments and personnel turnover-issues that also affect the security industry.

Many of the examples and drills described in the book are centered on the fictional XYZ Corporation. The majority of the scenar ios are geared toward a corporate headquarters or commercial office building. That does not mean that the principles and techniques described are not equally adaptable to a hospital, college, hotel, manufacturing plant, or other environment. Some readers may take issue with the procedures described in the drills. The purpose of the book is to explain the concepts of practical training and not to teach emergency response drills. Different facilities will have different needs and use different policies and procedures for dealing with various situations. The reader should focus on the concepts and techniques and tailor them to meet the requirements at their facility.

The book is organized to introduce the reader to the principles of practical training and illustrate several methods for implementing these principles. The reader should endeavor to adopt what is applicable and useful to their situation. Methods of testing and evaluating the program's effectiveness are included as is a list that may be useful to trainers.

I would like to thank the numerous people who have influenced, inspired, and supported me in the writing of this book, including the many instructors, leaders, and peers in the Marine Corps who introduced me to concepts like "fog of war" and "commander's intent" and taught me the importance of simulating fluid situations and maintaining an unconventional mindset; the staff at Butterworth–Heinemann, especially Laurel DeWolf and Rita Lombard; the professional managers and staff at Guardsmark; the ASIS members who provided me with input and suggestions on penetration testing; my sister-in-law, Cathy, who helped with some of the typing and computer applications; my parents, who always supported and encouraged me; and especially my wife, Christina, for all her patience and support.

# Introduction to Practical Security Training

Terrorist bombings at New York's World Trade Center, the Alfred Murrah Federal Building in Oklahoma City, and the Olympic Park in Atlanta; mass shootings by disgruntled employees in their workplaces; thefts of billions of dollars in high-tech equipment and proprietary information—in today's modern world, corporations, government agencies, hospitals, and schools face a wide new range of threats. In response to this new array of threats, the organization must respond by deploying a competent and professional security force to protect its assets. Assets encompass physical property, personnel, and information.

Developing an effective security force is not as simple as it may seem. Organizations not only have to properly screen and select personnel, they must also ensure that proper, effective, and cost-efficient training is conducted to prepare those personnel to face a wide range of challenges. This training must be geared to involve the student and test his/her ability to respond to a given situation. Too often training is insufficient or nonexistent in the private sector because many companies believe it to be too costly. Additional factors such as high employee turnover and small profit margins within the contract security services market make extensive training difficult. Many proprietary security forces face dwindling budgets and are often seen as a necessary evil, not a profit center, for the organization.

Suffice it to say, the majority of private sector security personnel do not receive even a fraction of the training that their counterparts in the military and public law enforcement agencies receive. To remedy this, security managers must adopt an aggressive, proactive approach to educating and developing the members of their security force. Training must be made interesting, realistic, and practical. Fortunately, with the proper mindset and a little imagination, this is achievable.

Public sector law enforcement personnel usually attend an academy for initial training. This training is a full-time pursuit, usually lasting between three and six months. Following initial training, most personnel will receive periodic refresher courses or specialized training at their agency's expense. Military personnel performing security duties normally have completed three months of basic training followed by schools of varying length related to their job specialty. All of this training has been residential in nature and very intensive.

Private security personnel generally receive training ranging from a few hours to one week. Much of this training is on-the-job and varies in quality. Some states are now mandating a prescribed number of hours of training following a set curriculum. For example, New York State, under the Security Guard Act of 1992, requires eight hours of preassignment training and 16 hours of on-the-job training within a period of 90 days after employment has begun. Additionally, eight hours of in-service training are required annually. While this is only 24 hours of training, and the curriculum is very basic, many states have no requirements at all. Most employers, both proprietary and contract, conduct some sort of site-specific training to orient the new employee to his or her job. This often follows no standard format and consists of an existing employee, usually with no background as a trainer, walking the new person through the policies and procedures at the particular facility. To make matters worse, there is usually no quality control and no attempt is made to evaluate the effectiveness of the training. Problems in the training may become obvious for the first time when an incident occurs and the employee responds incorrectly or inadequately.

This is not to say that there are not organizations within the private sector that have excellent training programs, but they tend to be the exception, not the rule. One security services company that provides armed security personnel to government agencies, runs a two-week residential training course for new employees, and many security companies with Department of Energy contracts are required to administer training that is quite similar to that given by public sector agencies. Again, however, this is the exception.

I recently attended an awards ceremony for security officers who demonstrated exceptional courage during a shooting spree that occurred at New York's Empire State Building. This ceremony drove home the kinds of threats that relatively (in comparison with their public sector counterparts) untrained security personnel may face. While the Empire State Building incident is certainly not an everyday occurrence, acts of workplace violence and domestic terrorism are on the rise and the chance that private security personnel may be confronted with these incidents is increasing. And it is not only the exceptionally dramatic threats that security personnel must prepare to face. Medical emergencies, fires, and incidents involving emotionally disturbed persons all take place with disturbing regularity and all call for a response by a prepared, well-trained force.

This book is designed to be a guide for security managers and security trainers who are seeking to improve the quality and professionalism of their security force, but are faced with time and budgetary constraints. Building good, effective training into the regular schedule of the security operation will not only reduce the risk of an incident occurring and minimize the effects of incidents which do occur, but will also, with proper documentation, reduce the liability to the organization.

Many of the training techniques and methods described within this book were borrowed from the military, particularly the Marine Corps. As mentioned earlier, the military, like public sector law enforcement agencies, has a structured and formal training process.

However, the need exists to maintain proficiency through constant training while also meeting other commitments. In this regard the military has done a very effective job of integrating practical training in an environment of too little time and too many commitments—the same environment many security organizations find themselves in.

While this book is directed primarily toward training uniformed guard forces, the same principles and some of the same techniques may be applied to the training of investigators, executive protection personnel, and others involved in the security function. By introducing "walk through, talk through" exercises, individual skills testing, emergency response drills, role-play, case study review, and hypothetical problem solving, security management can direct subordinates to view their job in a whole new way. Even organizations that may be utilizing some of these techniques may discover new applications and methods to bring out the best in their security force.

# 2

# *Practical versus Theoretical Training*

For many organizations, formal training consists simply of lectures; an instructor stands in front of the class and discusses theoretical concepts, sometimes simply reading aloud from a book or prepared notes. Heads bob, people fight to stay focused (the motivated people, that is—the others simply surrender to the desire to sleep), students plan their weekend or daydream about being somewhere else. The instructor may recognize this but accepts it as simply expected. The topics the instructor is discussing—things like how to respond to a fire or medical emergency—are not getting through to most of the employees in the class.

This is not to say that lecture is not important. Lecture based training is a necessary and key component of most training programs. Employees need a foundation of knowledge to work with and the best way to present these concepts initially is in a lecture format. This is also not intended to imply that all lecturers are boring and simply read from prepared notes, there are many exciting, dynamic, and motivated instructors. Most people are familiar with the above scenario, however, and training stops here. The security employees may understand the basic concepts, but they don't really see how it affects them

5

For training to be effective, it must be relevant. The student must understand the concepts the instructor is presenting and recognize how they will effect him or her in the course of their daily duties. It may seem like common sense to say that a member of a security department should recognize the dangers he or she would face if a fire occurred at their facility. However, if the student is simply given information about fire (i.e., the classes of fire, stages of fire, and so on) and some basic guidelines for combating it (i.e., call 911, employ fire extinguishers) he may intellectually understand the information, but unless he has actually experienced a fire, the relevance may not sink in.

How can this training become relevant to the inexperienced employee or the employee who has never faced this particular threat? Illustrate the situation by describing an incident that actually happened (case study) or developing a scenario based on specific factors at the employee's organization that will allow the employee to vividly picture him- or herself confronted with the problem (hypothetical scenario). Case studies and hypothetical scenarios, both of which are discussed later in this book, are two good tools to make training relevant. These are both methods that can be used in a classroom environment and do not require a great deal of equipment or coordination. The instructor must simply take the time to research the case study or devise the hypothetical scenario and present it to the class.

The key in both situations is involving the student in the training. The student is placed in a situation where he or she is forced to consider how they would respond to that particular threat or crisis. Often, particularly when the class is small in size, discussion of this sort of situation will inspire one of the students to mention a similar situation he or she faced and how the situation was resolved. This sort of participation is a good indicator that the training is achieving its desired goal of involving the students. Unfortunately, it can be difficult to achieve this level of participation in larger classes. Forced participation is almost never a good idea. Singling out students in a large class, like your third-grade teacher used to do, is a surefire way to raise the tension level in the class and inhibit learning. This is particularly true of adult learners in a group of their coworkers. The focus will immediately shift from understanding the material being presented to becoming as inconspicuous as possible. The only real exception is when the training is designed to force decision making under stressful conditions. This is a very important type of training, which will be discussed later, but that is not generally applicable in a classroom setting, particularly with a large class.

A good way to achieve many of the same results with a larger class is to split the class into small work groups of two to five people each. Give the work groups a project and then move among the groups to supervise and review what is being done. Another common tool is the role-play. Role-playing can be done in a classroom environment or in the field and in conjunction with another exercise such as a drill.

Outside of the classroom, there are many other techniques and training vehicles for involving the student. Emergency drills are an excellent way of allowing security personnel to actually respond as they would in a real crisis. This allows them an opportunity to see how a real response would be conducted and allows both them and management to identify problem areas and correct them. "Walk through, talk through" exercises are similar to drills but at a much slower pace and usually without much actual movement. They can best be described as playing through a hypothetical situation while actually walking the ground. In the military this is often called a TEWT, or Tactical Evolution Without Troops. This is discussed more extensively in a later chapter. The walk through, talk through exercise allows us to bring the hypothetical scenario training to a higher level without the coordination, and often expense, of a full-scale drill.

It is essential when training security personnel to understand and utilize the accepted techniques for teaching adult learners. According to Garry Mitchell, author of *The Trainer's Handbook: The AMA Guide to Effective Training* (1993, p. 23), there are ten recognized principles of adult education:

1. People learn only when they are ready to learn.
2. People learn best what they actually perform.
3. People learn from their mistakes.
4. People learn easiest what is familiar to them.

5. People favor different senses for learning.
6. People learn methodically and, in our culture, systematically.
7. People cannot learn what they cannot understand.
8. People learn through practice.
9. People learn better when they can see their own progress.
10. People learn best when what they are to learn is presented uniquely for them. Each of us is different.

While this book will attempt to embrace all these principles, there are some key points that will appear repeatedly through this text and are especially appropriate when considering practical security training.

*People learn only when they are ready to learn:* Training should proceed progressively so that the trainees' skills will improve and they will develop confidence.

*People learn best what they actually perform:* This is the underlying principle of practical training in a nutshell. There is a considerable difference between learning material in the classroom setting and understanding it theoretically versus actually physically performing tasks and applying techniques that have been learned. The goal of the security trainer should be to build a foundation through classroom instruction and other theoretical means and then introduce hands-on instruction to complete the training cycle. Once the initial training cycle is complete, practical training can be introduced as a method of evaluation and testing as well as reinforcement.

*People learn from their mistakes:* Mistakes can be very powerful tools for learning and can demonstrate important points to the trainee. Mistakes also allow the trainee to realize that everything will not always go according to plan and that minor mistakes will not necessarily result in total failure. The critique period following practical training exercises, such as emergency response drills, is an excellent opportunity to identify and learn from mistakes that occurred. In fact, one of the goals of practical training is to make mistakes in a controlled situation so that the likelihood of making the same mistakes in a real crisis is reduced. In this respect, mistakes in training should be viewed as a positive thing and an indication that the training is suitably challenging. A lack of mistakes or too smooth a response, particularly in the early stages of training, may be a sign that the training is not sufficiently challenging or realistic. The instructor should become concerned when the same mistakes are made repeatedly by the same trainees or when trainees refuse to acknowledge or take responsibility for their mistakes. When this occurs, the instructor may need to give more personalized attention to that student or students.

*People learn easiest what is familiar to them:* Throughout this book the importance of relevant training will be stressed. Security personnel must understand why something is important to them if they are to be expected to learn it well. If a security officer is assigned to a commercial office building and his or her primary responsibility is access control, the security officer will best relate and respond to training scenarios that involve access control in a commercial office building. If the trainee feels that the training is not relevant or is unrealistic he or she will not be as willing and ready to learn.

*People favor different senses for learning:* The goal of practical training is to immerse the trainee in a situation that resembles a real situation as closely as possible. This may mean creating an environment that closely resembles not only the sights but also the sounds, smells, and emotional feel of a real crisis.

*People learn methodically and, in our culture, systematically:* Training should be progressive and build upon itself. An example would be the following training cycle for a building evacuation:

1. *Classroom instruction:* Lecture on building evacuation techniques and evacuation procedures for the facility in question.

2. *Walk through, talk through exercise:* Trainees should be walked through the facility, shown different evacuation routes, and evacuation procedures taught in class should be reviewed.
3. *Evacuation Drill I:* Trainees are presented with a scenario requiring building evacuation. The trainees then conduct an evacuation with role-players acting as building employees.
4. *Evacuation Drill II:* As in the first drill, trainees are presented with a scenario requiring building evacuation. The trainees then conduct an evacuation with role-players acting as building employees. In this case, friction will be added to the drill. The trainer will announce a sudden power outage or will present the trainees with injured role-players or other scenarios that upset the normal flow of the drill and force the trainees to react appropriately.

*People learn through practice:* As the trainee repeats certain actions or responses, they become second nature and the trainee becomes more comfortable performing them. This can only lead to a more successful outcome when a real situation occurs.

*People learn better when they can see their own progress:* Checklists and critique sessions not only help the instructor, they assist the students as well. As the trainees see themselves improving, they gain greater confidence which in turn leads to greater improvement and learning.

*People respond best when what they are to learn is presented uniquely for them. Each of us is different:* In any learning situation individual attention and a low student-teacher ratio is key. The more the training can be specified and tailored to the individuals involved, the better the result will be. As with any type of leadership (and training is definitely a leadership situation), the trainer/leader must recognize that each of the trainees/subordinates is an individual and will respond to different stimulation or direction. Some trainees may willingly learn because they believe the trainer knows more and is trying to help them. Others may be more resistant, feel the training is unnecessary, or try to challenge the trainer's credibility. These situations may require a more persuasive and less autocratic style of leadership.

Practical training also can be beneficial for legal reasons. While the focus of this book is not on the legal ramifications of training programs, in our litigious society this aspect is worthy of mention. In the aftermath of a serious incident, when claims of negligent security are made by a plaintiff, the security training program is frequently called into question. Some key points that are often examined are listed here:

1. *Compliance with local regulations:* If there are state or city regulations pertaining to security officer training, have they been followed?
2. *Community and peer standards:* How does the training program compare to the training programs used by similar institutions in the same area?
3. *Relevance:* Are the skills taught to the security officers applicable to their duties at that location?
4. *Demonstration:* Does the training program involve the trainees demonstrating their ability to apply the skills they have been taught?
5. *Evaluation:* Is there testing in place to objectively evaluate the effectiveness of the training?
6. *Documentation:* Lesson plans, handouts, tests, and skills evaluation checklists should be kept on file.
7. *Continuity:* Training must be continuous. In addition to initial training and orientation, periodic refresher training is necessary; perishable skills must be practiced to be retained.
8. *Instructor qualifications:* Instructors must have the background to teach their subject matter and the ability to convey it effectively. Additionally, instructors must always be learning and

seeking professional improvement. The motto of the American Society for Law Enforcement Trainers is "Qui docet, discet" which means "Those who teach, learn." This is also an excellent motto for security instructors.

Several of these points are mentioned in "Training on Trial" by D. Anthony Nichter, CPP (September 1996, p. 75–78). Nichter's article does an excellent job of discussing the legal implications of a security training program. Court recognition of the importance of practical training is illustrated when Nichter cites a case where a security program was challenged because it was composed entirely of lecture. The court made the distinction between education and training, noting that the lecture-only program was purely education, not training. According to the court, training must require the students to practice the skills they are learning. The realization that the courts acknowledge the difference between training and education and look at practical skills training as a measure of competence should be a powerful impetus to implement a practical training program.

There are several general principles that make up the foundation of a practical security training program:

1. The training seeks to involve the student.
2. Training is relevant.
3. A building block approach is used to progressively improve the students' skills and knowledge.
4. Students demonstrate skills to illustrate competence.
5. Training is scenario based and made as realistic as possible.
6. Training seeks to simulate not only the physical aspects, but also the emotional and psychological elements of a crisis.
7. Training develops decision-making skills.
8. Trainees are encouraged to take the initiative, in keeping with the company's philosophy.
9. Training can be evaluated through both traditional means, such as written tests and skills demonstration, and through surprise drills and penetration testing.

10. Training is continuous and evolving. It constantly seeks to iden-
    tify weaknesses and areas for improvement and then addresses
    these issues.

Trainers adhering to these principles should see a significant
improvement in the performance of the security program. Of course,
training alone is never the entire solution. The security personnel
being trained must have the requisite intelligence, social skills, and
motivation to make the program successful. If those factors are
present, practical training can create a framework for building and
developing a more efficient and professional security force.

## REFERENCES

Mitchell, Garry. *The Trainer's Handbook: The AMA Guide to Effective Training.* New York: AMACOM, 1993, p. 23.

Nichter, D. Anthony. "Training on Trial." *Security Management*, September 1996, pp. 75–78.

# 3

# *Identifying the Training Needs of the Security Force*

Before a security manager can begin to attempt to create a more practical, realistic, and effective training program, he or she must first identify the needs of the security force at that particular organization. What kinds of problems are security personnel likely to confront and what are the proper procedures for dealing with them? What are the basic and advanced skills that the security staff need to acquire and maintain to respond to the relevant incidents and crises they may face? To answer these questions, the security manager and security trainer must look closely at their organization and the risks it faces.

If the security department has not already conducted a risk analysis of their organization, this is a good first step. While incidents such as fire and medical emergencies plague virtually every organization, many concerns are specific to the particular industry or sector to which the organization belongs. The threats that face an inner-city hospital may be very different from those faced by a financial institution with global operations. Likewise, the concerns of a large shopping mall or department store may not be the same as the concerns of a real estate management firm responsible for the operation of a high-rise commercial office building. The types of threats will dictate the focus of emergency response training for security. The security manager or trainer should use the probability/criticality model when evaluating the threats to his or her organization. In this model, the manager evaluates each threat the organization faces and considers two points: (1) How likely is the event to take place? (2) How critical of an impact will the event have on the organization if it does take place? For example: A security manager for a major financial institution with thousands of employees considers the theft of a laptop computer from the company's offices. What is the probability of this event occurring? Pretty high, unfortunately, especially within a large company. While he or she would hope this was not a daily occurrence, it is a fairly common event. What is the criticality of the event? Assuming the laptop does not contain a wealth of valuable proprietary information, probably not that high. It is a loss of several thousand dollars to an institution that functions in terms of millions or billions of dollars. What if the same manager were to consider the threat of someone driving a vehicle loaded with explosives into the building's subterranean parking garage or parking in front of the building and detonating the explosives? Probability? Well, it certainly has happened, most notably in the United States at the World Trade Center in New York in 1993 and the Alfred Murrah Federal Building in Oklahoma City in 1995. But it certainly is not one of the more common crises a security manager must face. Criticality? Incredible, particularly if it happens during working hours when employees are in the facility. The cost in human life alone would probably be staggering. Security management must take these considerations into account not only when establishing training programs, but also when deploying all of their assets.

Once the probable threats and incidents have been identified, a training program can be developed to prepare the staff to face these challenges. By using practical training methods such as drills, the security staff can learn to confront these problems on a practical level as well as having an intellectual understanding of the problem. How training will be carried out will depend not only on the resourcefulness of the trainer, but also on the culture and philosophy of the organization.

Ideally, every organization should have a security procedures manual that serves as a guideline for the operations of the security force. This manual is the foundation for the development of site-specific training. The manual, generally, should be divided into five parts:

1. Contact information for key building personnel, contractors, vendors and, of course, security department personnel
2. Post orders for each security post at the facility
3. Emergency response procedures covering most anticipated situations that may arise
4. General guidelines and standards of conduct for security personnel
5. An appendix covering examples of paperwork used and other information not included in the other sections of the manual

The two sections of the manual most relevant to training are sections two and three. The post orders section describes how the security officer deals with daily tasks such as access control and patrol. This can be used as a guideline to test the security officer's ability to perform daily functions that are not necessarily emergency response-related. Two examples of this type of training are the testing of the security officer's observation skills and a penetration testing exercise of the access control at the facility. Both of these types of training will be discussed later in the book. The emergency procedures section of the manual provides guidelines for responding to various types of incidents that may reasonably be anticipated to occur. There are some types of emergencies that should definitely be included in every manual, such as fire and medical emergency procedures. These are incidents which could occur at virtually any facility. Some other procedures may be more specific to the particular site. For example, in a high-rise building, procedures for responding to an elevator entrapment should be included. Likewise, a hospital security manual should include procedures for dealing with emotionally disturbed persons.

Once the manual has been developed, it can serve as a guideline for site-specific training exercises. The new employee should be given an opportunity to familiarize him- or herself with the contents and then the manual should be accessible so that it may be used as a reference by security officers on post. The manual should be located where it can be referenced when necessary, but it should not be so widely distributed that the security procedures of the facility are compromised. As procedures and policies are changed and revised, the manual must be updated accordingly. If the security manager wanted to test the ability of the security force to respond to a particular type of emergency, he or she could create a scenario and conduct a drill. The manual could then be used as a measuring stick to determine how closely the procedures were followed. Conversely, the drill may allow the security manager to identify weaknesses in the procedures and the manual can be modified accordingly.

The security manager may wish to create a separate training manual in addition to the security procedures manual. The training manual could be disseminated to each new member of the security staff, thereby giving staff member a ready-reference guide that is relatively free of sensitive information that could compromise the organization's security. The security department may also consider separating general task training from specialist and team training. For example, a set of standards for training may be developed for individual skills that all members of the security force should possess, and a separate set of standards could be created for specialist personnel within the security force. Examples of specialist personnel would include investigators, drivers, emergency medical technicians, console operators, executive protection personnel, fire safety personnel, and security receptionists. A third set of standards could be developed for teams within the security force. This would not only concentrate on the individual skills possessed by each member, but also on their ability to function as a group, a critical factor for success in emergency situations.

By putting all these components together, the security manager can begin to create a training program that will develop a staff prepared to deal with situations that may occur at that particular facility. The development and use of a security procedures manual is a key part of this strategy.

While no security manual can possibly cover every single contingency that may occur, using it as a training aid will help create a mindset in the members of the security force that will assist them in dealing with even unforeseen situations. In the military this is referred to as understanding the "commander's intent." The concept is that when an operation order is given to troops prior to an operation, the order includes not only specific instructions, but the intent behind them. Therefore, when things begin to fall apart and the plan goes out the window, the junior leader will be able to adapt and will still accomplish the mission because he or she understands the commander's intent. This concept is very applicable in the security field. Emergency situations often arise during off-hour shifts, when senior members of the security department are not on site. Junior leaders such as shift supervisors and console operators must often make timely decisions while an attempt is being made to notify the senior leadership. If these personnel have been trained in decision-making and understand the intent and the philosophy of the senior leadership, the chances for a successful resolution to the problem are much greater.

After these steps have been taken and a comprehensive site-specific security training program has been developed, it can become an invaluable aid not only for training and evaluation, but also for identifying personnel suitable for promotion. Promotion can be contingent upon completion of certain phases of individual and specialist training and for filling leadership roles in team training exercises. This will allow the security department an effective, measurable, and independent way to identify and choose its leaders.

The following is an example of a site-specific training program outline:

1. *Orientation outline:* This is an outline of topics for the training officer to cover with each new member of the security department. This should indicate the number of hours of instruction for each topic. The topics should focus on both general security topics and post procedures. These should be followed by training in emergency response procedures. There should be

space on the outline for both the training officer and the new employee to initial upon completion of each segment.

2. *Orientation manual:* This should be a relatively brief manual to assist the new employee undergoing training. It should be a ready reference on both general topics and post duties but should not be so detailed that it would jeopardize security if it was lost.

3. *Postorientation evaluation:* This should be a brief written examination, perhaps accompanied by a demonstration of some skills learned during the orientation period. This will ensure that the orientee learned and retained the body of knowledge necessary to assume post.

4. *Individual skills training:* This should be a set of standards for skills that each member of the security force needs to possess. These skills should be tested and evaluated through practical application on a regular basis. These skills will include what the employee learned in orientation training.

5. *Specialist skill training:* This should be a set of standards for skills possessed by designated members of the security force. These individuals will possess not only the individual skills that all members of the security force must demonstrate, but also will have skills related to a specialized job such as console operator, driver, or investigator.

6. *Team skills training:* This will be a set of standards for team operations. This can refer to specialized teams within the security force, shift teams, or any other group within the security department that has to function as a unit. This also is a good opportunity to train and evaluate the team leaders.

7. *Leadership training:* In addition to the training and evaluation that occurs during team training, the junior leaders can also be trained separately. Some effective methods are through hypothetical scenarios and walk through, talk through exercises, which are described at length later in the book. This type of training focuses on decision-making and judgment, two critical areas for leadership positions.

When developing the orientation outline, the security manager must consider what general and site-specific topics are required knowledge for every member of the security force. Then the period of time to be spent on each subject should be determined. The following illustration depicts an example of an orientation outline that can be used for training security personnel working in a commercial office building. Table 3–1 illustrates an example of a forty-hour orientation and initial training program. This checklist would be completed by the trainer as the student completes each phase.

**Table 3–1.** Orientation for Security Staff

| Subject/Post | Number of Hours | Date of Training | Initials of Trainee | Initials of Trainer |
|---|---|---|---|---|
| Access Control | 2 | | | |
| Emergency Response | 2 | | | |
| Legal Powers | 2 | | | |
| Report Writing | 1 | | | |
| Public Relations | 1 | | | |
| Ethics and Conduct | 1 | | | |
| Post 1 Main Lobby | 7 | | | |
| Post 2 Reception | 6 | | | |
| Post 3 Freight | 4 | | | |
| Post 4 Floor Patrol | 6 | | | |
| Post 5 Perimeter Patrol | 4 | | | |
| Post 6 Relief/ Response | 4 | | | |
| Total Hours | 40 | | | |

An important component of the orientation process can be the employee orientation manual. This manual will give the security trainee a ready reference to carry during the training period and during subsequent assignment to the facility. The manual should give a brief description of the facilities, important phone extensions, a basic description of the posts, and a list of key personnel. This document should be carefully reviewed before dissemination to ensure that it does not provide too much information. If the orientation manual is too descriptive it may assist an outsider to breach the building's security should it fall into the wrong hands. This is something that can only be determined by the security director or security manager at that specific location. Following is an example of an outline for a security orientation manual:

1. *Introduction:* Describes manual and states its purpose
2. *Description of facility:* Gives a physical description of the building or buildings that comprise the facility. If the organization has several locations they can be combined in one manual, or separate manuals can be developed for each site.
3. *Description of posts:* As detailed as the security department feels is prudent
4. *Description of policies:* An overview on policies regarding access control, property removal, and emergency response. Again, the security department will want to determine the depth of the description.
5. *Contact information:* Internal extensions for key departments and vendor contact numbers (i.e., elevator repair, glaziers, plumbers, electricians)
6. *Key personnel:* The names of key contact people within the organization. This will help prevent embarrassing situations when new employees may be unfamiliar with the names of key people. Contact information for each person should be kept in the main security procedures manual on post, not within the orientation manual.
7. *General standards of conduct:* A description of what is expected of each member of the security department in terms of appearance, public relations, and personal conduct is outlined.

Following the completion of the orientation/training period for new security personnel, an evaluation should be conducted to ensure that the training was effective. This is a common theme of the concept of practical training. The need for evaluation will be stressed repeatedly throughout this text. The evaluation should consist of two parts: a brief written examination and a demonstration of individual skills. The written examination should consist of a review of procedures, key personnel, facility layout, and so on. The following is an example of written exam questions for a typical commercial office building facility:

1. What are the normal hours of operation for the building?
   a. 6:00 A.M. to 7:00 P.M.
   b. 8:00 A.M. to 6:00 P.M.
   c. 7:00 A.M. to 7:00 P.M.
   d. 9:00 A.M. to 5:00 P.M.
2. When a person enters the building and claims to have lost his/her I.D. card, the appropriate response is to:
   a. Refuse entry to the person.
   b. Refer the person to the reception desk.
   c. Call the person's supervisor.
   d. If you recognize the person, allow access.
3. If a telephone bomb threat is received, you should:
   a. Immediately evacuate the building.
   b. Gather as much information as possible and notify the security manager or supervisor.
   c. Gather as much information as possible and notify the floors via the public address system.
   d. Ignore the threat—98 percent of bomb threats are hoaxes.
4. The Chief Financial Officer of XYZ corporation is:
   a. John Jones.
   b. Steve Smith.
   c. Leonard Benotz.
   d. Edward Williams.
5. If an alarm is received at the east gate, the console operator should:

    a. Check the appropriate CCTV monitor prior to dispatching security personnel to investigate.

    b. Notify the security officer nearest to the alarm point to investigate.

    c. Dispatch a team of two security officers to investigate.

    d. Notify police and await their arrival.

6. When trucks are leaving the facility, the security officer assigned to the freight booth should:

    a. Inspect every truck for possible stolen company property.

    b. Inspect every truck, except those with seals.

    c. Inspect every truck, except those of regular vendors.

    d. Inspect trucks at random.

7. If someone is leaving the building with a box and refuses to show a property pass you should:

    a. Physically block him/her from exiting.

    b. Lock the door, preventing the person from leaving.

    c. Ask the person for an employee ID or business card and make a note of the incident.

    d. Call the police and tell them the person just stole something from the building.

8. When patrolling office spaces after hours, the security officer finding people in the offices should:

    a. Request to see their IDs and make a note on the patrol report.

    b. Move quietly through the area and not disturb them.

    c. Greet them, but do not challenge them.

    d. Request that they display ID and ask them why they are on the floor at that time.

9. When the lobby security officer receives a notification of an elevator entrapment, he/she should:

    a. Notify building engineering and resume normal duties.

    b. Notify engineering and attempt to maintain communication with the occupants throughout the entrapment.

    c. Attempt to bring the elevator to the lobby with the fire recall procedure.

   d. Take the elevator bank out of service and call the fire department
10. When confronted with a hostile person who may be emotionally disturbed, you should:
   a. Tell the person to get out of the building immediately, and notify a supervisor about the incident.
   b. Try to calm the person and move the conversation to a quieter area while notifying a supervisor.
   c. Call for immediate help from the reaction force.
   d. Ask the person to step into a more secluded area so that you can speak one to one.

This is just a brief selection of the types of questions that can be used for a site-specific written exam. Some questions deal with specific policies, some test the trainee's response to various situations using the organization's policies, and some test knowledge of key personnel and building operations. The length of the test will be determined largely by the size of the facility and the extent of the duties. Generally, twenty-five to fifty questions is a good length. Multiple choice is the quickest, easiest format to grade. Some managers and trainers also may want to include questions that require brief written answers.

The written exam is the first step to ensuring that initial training has been successful. The second step is a brief inventory of skills learned during orientation. In this phase, the security manager, trainer, or some other senior evaluator from the security department should accompany the trainee to the various posts he/she has been trained on and observe a demonstration of the basic skills required for each post. An example of this sort of skill inventory follows:

1. Main Gate:
   a. Demonstrate checking vehicle sticker.
   b. Demonstrate verifying vehicle without sticker.
   c. Demonstrate inspecting departing vehicle.
2. Front Lobby:
   a. Demonstrate checking employee ID.

   b. Demonstrate checking visitor's pass.
   c. Demonstrate checking property removal pass.
3. Lobby Reception:
   a. Demonstrate use of computer system.
   b. Demonstrate issuance of visitor pass.
4. Loading Dock:
   a. Demonstrate knowledge of parking procedures for trucks.
   b. Demonstrate verification of contractors.
   c. Demonstrate issuance of contractor's pass.
5. Fire Command Station:
   a. Demonstrate acknowledging an alarm.
   b. Demonstrate use of PA system.
   c. Demonstrate use of warden phone.
   d. Demonstrate fire department liaison.
6. Interior Patrol:
   a. Demonstrate knowledge of areas to patrol.
   b. Demonstrate patrol of a floor.
   c. Demonstrate patrol of a stairwell.

For each of these areas, a brief checklist can be devised to allow the evaluator to determine if the trainee has a comprehension of his or her duties and can carry them out effectively. This can be used as in-service training, as part of a larger training exercise, or as a qualifying stage for promotion.

## REFERENCE

*U.S. Marine Corps Battle Drill Guide: Individual Training Standards Occupational Field 03 Infantry*. Marine Corps Institute, Marine Barracks, Washington, D.C., June 1988.

# 4

# Use of Case Studies in Training

One of the most valuable resources that the security manager or trainer has in creating scenarios for drills, problem-solving exercises, and other training is the case study. Case studies allow security personnel to review a situation that actually occurred and try to decide:

1. How could the situation have been handled better?
2. How would they react and what action would they take in a similar situation?
3. Was the situation preventable? How could it have been prevented?

Case studies have some advantages over hypothetical problem-based scenarios, which will be discussed later. Since case studies are events that have already occurred it is more difficult for them to be challenged as "unrealistic" and they are more likely to be taken seriously by trainees. The difficulty with case studies is that they require time to locate and research and they may not necessarily conform to the situation at the particular organization.

Case studies can be used in several ways.

1. *General classroom training:* Case studies can be used in lecture-based training to illustrate different points being taught. In this use, the case study does not necessarily have to conform to conditions at the organization, it can be used simply as a teaching aid.
2. *Response drills:* Situations that occurred at locations similar to that of the organization can be used to develop response drills. The facts of the case study can be used to create a scenario for the drill. If the participants are aware that the scenario is adapted from a real situation, it will have much greater impact on them.
3. *Basis for hypothetical situations:* This is discussed more extensively in Chapter 4. In some situations, a hypothetical scenario may be preferable. A case study can still form the basis of this scenario.

Using case studies in lecture-based training is very similar to any history class. Professionals in every field learn a great deal by studying the successes and failures of their peers and predecessors. This training can be conducted at various levels: for the basic security officer, for the supervisor, and for the manager. Some scenarios may be applicable to all levels, and some may be specific to a certain level of authority. Scenarios can be tailored to deal with almost any type of security problem from access control to workplace violence. Some cases may deal simultaneously with several problems or concerns. For example, the explosion of an improvised explosive device in a commercial office building will result in the need to consider:

1. Response to a medical emergency
2. Response to a fire
3. Crowd control
4. Evacuation procedures
5. Dealing with media representatives
6. Report writing
7. Crime scene containment

8. Access control (how did the device get into the building?)
9. Liaison with public agencies, such as law enforcement and emergency services

From this one case study we are able to identify nine separate issues that may need to be addressed.

One question most trainers have about case studies is how to find them. There are several sources that are readily and non-so-readily available. A good place to begin is the organization's own incident report archives. By reviewing past incident reports, the trainer can learn about situations that have already occurred at the facility and how they were dealt with. These scenarios can be replayed as training sessions. Sometimes the incident report archive may not prove to be a sufficient source of case studies. Another possible source is newspaper reports—major incidents are usually covered in the press. The trainer can create a clipping file as incidents occur and use them later as case studies. Unfortunately, newspaper reports rarely provide the type of detail necessary for a good case study. A better source may be trade periodicals like *Security Management*. This magazine often gives in-depth information about various incidents that have occurred and does so from a security perspective. Using a clipping file of these articles, the trainer can create an outline and frame the incident in the context of his or her organization.

Not only can case studies form the basis for drills and other exercises, but they also can be used to develop the decision-making skills of supervisors and other junior leaders. This can be done in a classroom setting as well as during a practical application exercise. The situations can be presented to the trainees in several formats:

1. *Small discussion group:* The supervisors discuss the situation among themselves and decide on a course of action.
2. *One-on-one:* The trainer presents the scenario to a supervisor or other junior leader and they describe the course of action they would take.

3. *Essay or written solution:* The trainees are given the problem in a classroom setting. Each trainee writes his or her response independent of the others.
4. *Panel:* A group composed of trainers and managers presents the case study to a trainee. The trainee then describes a course of action. This can also be used as a part of a promotion process.

In each of these formats, a critical element is the critique. The trainer should review the answer given and try to point out the strengths and weaknesses of the course of action described. The supervisor will then have an opportunity to evaluate how the trainee reached his or her decision. This process may seem tedious, but it will prove worthwhile if the end result is a supervisory group that can think and act independently when necessary.

An excellent example of a case study being used to educate security professionals is found in Major Charles E. Locke, Jr.'s article "Hostage Seizure in Peru: What Lessons for the Marine Security Guard" published in the November 1998 edition of the *Marine Corps Gazette*. In this article Major Locke recounts the December 1996 seizure of the Japanese ambassador's residence in Lima, Peru by members of the Tupac Amaru Revolutionary Movement. The assault occurred during a social function attended by several hundred people. The terrorists were able to enter the function disguised as members of the catering staff and held numerous hostages of many nationalities for over four months until Peruvian commandos stormed the residence and ended the situation.

Locke points out that if the attack had been directed at a U.S. diplomatic function, Marine Security Guards would have been involved, thereby making it relevant to the reader. He goes on to detail lessons learned for Marine Security Guards assigned to U.S. embassies and consulates around the globe—and in fact, lessons that are valuable to anyone providing security in a high-risk environment. Locke studied the Peruvian hostage drama from the planning stage to the conclusion of the crisis. He identified five key points for Marine Security Guards to focus on and learn from. These lessons apply to most security professionals, especially those working abroad. The points, paraphrased, are:

1. Develop security awareness—always recognize your vulnerabilities.
2. Recognize behavior that may indicate a threat. When operating abroad, language and cultural skills are of great value.
3. Recognize that dangers may not be apparent. Expect the unexpected.
4. Avoid patterns and routines while concentrating on security fundamentals.
5. Recognize that terrorists will use unconventional means and will not necessarily share your views of ethics, morality, or fairness.

Major Locke's article is one of the best examples of a security practitioner taking a case study and turning it into a relevant training tool.

Following are some examples of case studies for various types of incidents and their sources. These case studies should give the trainer some ideas as to the type and variety of scenarios that can be used and the sources that are available. The case studies described in this book are relatively brief, but the trainer can make the case study as detailed or as brief as is desirable. In some cases the depth will be limited by the amount of information available. Case studies can be another tool to make training more realistic and timely and enhance the capability of the security force.

## EXECUTIVE PROTECTION

Alfred Herrhausen, chairman of Deutsche Bank, was killed by a roadside bomb as he was driven to work on November 30, 1989. Herrhausen was riding in the center car of a three-car convoy, with bodyguards in both the lead and rear cars. The bomb was located 300 yards from his home and was concealed in a knapsack on a bicycle left in the street. The bomb was initiated by the interruption of a beam from a photoelectric cell, a method that greatly improved the accuracy and effectiveness of the attack. Source: "A Calculated Assassination," by Anthony Scotti, *Security Management*, November 1990.

The focus of a case study of this sort would be on prevention. Many kidnappings and assassinations occur when the victim is en route. Even if the route is varied, two locations are generally constant: home and work. Keeping this in mind, the trainer could ask the students:

1. How could the likelihood of this sort of attack be reduced?
2. What role would route variance have?
3. Could a route reconnaissance have detected this ambush?

## TRESPASSER/INTRUDER

The setting was the headquarters of a corporation located in a major urban area. The company had very lax procedures for screening visitors due to the nature of its business. One afternoon the security office received a phone call from a floor receptionist. The receptionist reported that several employees had complained of a young man entering their offices inquiring about working for the company. The man was directed to the floor receptionist, who gave him an application. The man completed the application, returned it to the receptionist, and left the floor. A few minutes later, the receptionist received a call from yet another employee stating that the man had been in her office, but had left and was now elsewhere in the building. At that point, the receptionist contacted the security office. The security staff began a thorough sweep of the floors and stairwells. With the assistance of closed circuit cameras monitored in the security console, the man was located in an elevator lobby on one of the floors and escorted from the building without incident. It was later determined that the man had been able to enter the office spaces on many of the floors because employees had propped open card-access-operated doors. The culture of the company also contributed to the failure to screen visitors and control their movements within the building. Source: incident report files.

Using this case study, the trainer can ask the students to consider the following points:

1. How could an employee security awareness program have restricted the movements of this person?
2. What methods were used and what methods could be used to locate a suspected intruder?
3. Role-play dealing with the intruder when he is located.
4. How could the application the man completed be used by security during and after the incident?

This sort of drill, particularly if the removal of the trespasser is role-played, can be very desirable in terms of teaching security personnel to deal with unauthorized or troubled individuals in a safe and effective way. A later chapter will give more attention to the use of role-playing in training.

## MASS SHOOTING/ARMED INTRUDER (SECURE FACILITY)

While the Capitol Building in Washington, DC, is open to the public, visitors must pass through security checkpoints equipped with metal detectors and manned by armed Capitol Police. At 3:40 P.M., 41-year-old Russell Weston, Jr. entered the Document Room entrance on the east side of the building. Weston attempted to bypass the metal detector and gain access to the building. Veteran Capitol Police Officer Jacob Chestnut attempted to stop him. Weston immediately drew a .38 caliber Smith & Wesson revolver and shot Chestnut in the head. Weston then began running toward a busy part of the building known as the crypt. At this point Weston exchanged gunfire with another Capitol Police officer before turning into a suite of offices occupied by House majority whip Tom DeLay and his staff. Special Agent John Gibson of the Capitol Police was assigned to DeLay's protective detail. He was in the office when Weston burst in, and he ordered Weston to drop his weapon. Weston fired, wounding Gibson, and Gibson returned fire, striking Weston in the leg and causing him to drop his gun. DeLay rushed in and directed several of his staffers to safety. Additional Capitol Police burst into the office and subdued Weston. The Capitol Police then directed employees and tourists to remain in the offices with the doors locked. The entrances to the building were sealed and the police conducted a room-by-room search to ensure that there were no other shooters. Both Chestnut and Gibson died of their wounds. Source: "Shooting in the Capitol," by Nancy Gibbs, *Time* magazine, August 3, 1998.

This case study depicts the difficulty of dealing with a determined armed assailant. Even though the Capitol had security checkpoints with metal detectors and armed guards, a violent intruder was able to gain access to the building by killing the guard at the security checkpoint. Lessons can be learned by reviewing how the Capitol Police, even after Weston was subdued, considered the possibility of one or more accomplices and kept the employees and tourists secured in offices while the police searched the building. The following questions could be used when discussing the situation with members of the security staff:

1. Could a repositioning of the checkpoint have reduced the ability of a determined attacker to gain entrance to the core of the building?
2. What did Special Agent John Gibson do correctly when engaging Weston?
3. What did the Capitol Police do correctly after subduing Weston?

## MASS SHOOTING/ARMED INTRUDER (PUBLIC FACILITY)

The Empire State Building is a world renowned symbol of New York City. While its primary function is as an office building, it is also a major tourist attraction. On any given day it is packed with tourists. Shortly after 5:00 P.M. on February 23, 1997, Ali Abu Kamal, a 69-year-old Palestinian former teacher from the Gaza Strip began firing a .380 caliber Beretta pistol on the eighty-sixth-floor observation deck. The observation deck is open to the public and anyone purchasing a ticket can gain access. Metal detectors had been used previously, in the wake of the World Trade Center bombing, but were removed after four months because of delays they caused. Kamal was reportedly angry at the United States and despondent over losing his $300,000 savings. Apparently Kamal waited in line for half an hour. When he got to the observation deck, a Belgian businessman claimed he heard Kamal approaching people and inquiring if they were Egyptian. Almost immediately afterwards, he drew the semiautomatic Beretta from beneath a long coat and began shooting randomly. The bullets struck seven people, killing one. Kamal then turned the gun on himself. Source: "The Empire State Horror," by Corky Siemaszko, *New York Daily News*, February 24, 1997, and "He Cased Slay Site on Saturday," by Alice McQuillan, et. al., *New York Daily News*, February 25, 1997.

This case demonstrates the difficulty of protecting people in a public area. Metal detectors were reinstalled following this incident. The following questions could be used when discussing this case:

1. How could a security staff member assigned to the observation deck have responded without endangering themselves?
2. In the aftermath of an incident of this sort, how could security personnel reduce panic, regain control of the crowd, and assist emergency services personnel responding?

## WORKPLACE VIOLENCE

On December 6, 1989, Marc Lepine, 25 years old, entered the L'Ecole Polytechnique at the University of Montreal. Stepping from a stairwell onto the second floor, Lepine entered a classroom and drew a semiautomatic rifle from a bag he was carrying. There were fifty male students and ten female students in the classroom. Lepine separated them and ordered the male students to leave. When the men left, Lepine fired at the group of female students, killing six. He then left the classroom and rampaged through several floors of the school, shooting at students. After killing a total of fourteen people and wounding thirteen, Lepine killed himself. Lepine was later identified as a rejected University applicant with a pattern of anger against women. In the aftermath of the incident, several problems were disclosed:

1. Lepine wandered the floors prior to the incident. Several students noticed he looked out of place, but he was not challenged or reported to security.
2. When 911 was called, misidentification of the building where the incident was occurring caused police to initially respond to the wrong building.
3. There was no way to contain or track Lepine's movement within the building. When the police first arrived, they had to wait for a SWAT team before entering the building.

Source: "Painful Lesson," by Floyd E. Phelps, CPP. *Security Management,* March 1995. The trainer could ask the following questions:

1. Could Lepine have been safely contained in any way after the shooting started?
2. How could students have been safely evacuated from the area?
3. How could communication with 911 have been improved?
4. Would a security escort have aided the police response?

## REFERENCES

Gibbs, Nancy. "Shooting in the Capitol." *Time,* August 3, 1998.

Locke, Major Charles E., Jr. "Hostage Seizure in Peru: What Lessons for the Marine Security Guard." *Marine Corps Gazette,* November 1998.

McQuillan, Alice, et. al. "He Cased the Slay Site on Saturday." *New York Daily News.* February 25, 1997.

Phelps, Floyd E. "Painful Lesson." *Security Management,* March 1995.

Scotti, Anthony. "A Calculated Assassination." *Security Management,* November 1990.

Siemaszko, Corky. "The Empire State Horror." *New York Daily News,* February 24, 1997.

# 5

# *Use of Hypothetical Situations in Training*

There may be times when it is difficult to find the appropriate case study or when the case studies do not translate well to the trainer's organization. In this case, a hypothetical scenario may be more suitable. When using a hypothetical scenario, the trainer should strive to be as realistic as possible. Even though a particular case study or historical example may not be used, it would be sensible for the trainer to familiarize him- or herself with factual situations that have occurred and are similar to the scenario.

The use of hypothetical situations for developing supervisors' decision-making skills was discussed earlier, and some examples were cited. Hypothetical situations can be presented to security officers as part of a formal training class, a promotion board, or a post inspection. The security staff member's responses will indicate several things:

1. *Judgment:* Can the person decide on a rational course of action under the circumstances?
2. *Knowledge of company security procedures:* Does the answer reflect a knowledge of the company's procedures? Not every situation will be covered in a procedures manual, but does the person take into account applicable procedures for similar sit-

uations or otherwise answer in the spirit, if not the letter, of company policy?

3. *Decision-making ability:* Is the person willing and able to make decisions in the absence of a supervisor or manager if necessary?
4. *Reasoning:* Can the person think through the problem in a methodical way to reach a solution?

Some hypothetical situations may test all of these elements, some may test only a few. Trainers should follow a progression beginning with more basic situations that are covered by security procedures and advance to more complex situations that require independent problem solving. Following are some examples of situations and possible questions that trainers can use to test their staff members.

## SAMPLE SCENARIOS

### Intruder

A middle-aged man in a suit enters the lobby of XYZ Corporation. He bypasses the reception area and goes straight to the elevator bank. He ignores the security officer's request to display ID and moves toward the elevators. What does the security officer do?

1. Does the company have a policy for dealing with this or a similar situation? Was this policy followed?
2. Did the security officer indicate that notification would be made to a supervisor?
3. Did the security officer consider abandoning post to follow the individual or dispatching someone else to follow the intruder?
4. Did the security officer consider shutting down the elevators? Would this be a viable option?

### Violent Incident Involving a Weapon

The security console operator receives a phone call from an employee on the tenth floor. The employee tells the console operator that there is a man carrying a pistol walking in and out of the offices on the floor. The man is believed to be a former employee named Pete Johnson.

1. Whom did the console operator notify?
2. Did the console operator make attempts to contain the situation?
3. Did the console operator know how his personal information could be gathered regarding Johnson? This might help the police in the event of a hostage situation.

## Property Removal

At 7:30 P.M., a well-dressed gentleman steps from the elevator carrying a computer processing unit in the manufacturer's box. The security officer in the lobby requests that the man produce a property pass signed by an authorized signatory. Additionally, because equipment is involved, serial numbers should be included on the pass. The gentleman explains that there is no one left upstairs to sign a property pass and that he is in a hurry. He then begins to move toward the exit.

1. Did the trainee understand and follow the company policy for property removal?
2. Did the trainee attempt to stop the man from leaving?
3. Did the trainee request that the man produce employee ID?
4. Did the trainee make proper notification?

## Visitor Communicating a Threat

A visitor approaches the XYZ company lobby reception desk, identifies himself as James Hubbard, and requests to see Paul Turner. The security officer on duty calls Mr. Turner's extension and informs him of the visitor. Mr. Turner tells the security officer to deny access to Mr. Hubbard and suggests that in the future he call in advance to schedule an appointment. The security officer then relays this information politely to Hubbard. The visitor becomes enraged, begins to curse at the security officer and says, "Someone ought to blow up this building with you in it!" Hubbard then walks angrily from the building.

1. What did the security officer do as soon as Hubbard left?
2. To whom was the situation reported?
3. Did the security officer know who could be contacted to provide more information on Hubbard and his background?

### Employee Stalking Victim

A female employee, Janet Wilson, approaches the lobby security supervisor and complains that an unknown man has been following her from the commuter train each day and has made lewd comments to her. The man, who wears business attire, usually rides in the same car of the train as the employee. The man then follows her from the train station to the XYZ corporate headquarters. She believes the man also works in the area. Despite her requests to stop bothering her, the man has persisted.

1. Does the security supervisor know whom to notify within the organization?
2. Does the supervisor indicate a need to contact the police?
3. Does the supervisor consider the possibility of providing an escort?
4. What other actions does the supervisor suggest?

### Theft

At 3:00 P.M. a call is received in the security console. The caller, an employee named Catherine Anderson, reports that her purse is missing. Ms. Anderson claims she left the purse under her desk to attend a meeting at 11:30 A.M. When the meeting ended at 2:30 P.M., Anderson returned to her desk to find the purse missing. After briefly searching the area, she concluded that it had been stolen.

1. Did the console operator dispatch a security officer to the floor to conduct a face-to-face interview with Ms. Anderson and take a report?

2. Did the security officer also interview other employees on the floor?
3. Did the console operator consider whether other assets such as CCTV or card-access system records could be used to assist in an investigation?
4. Did the console operator know whom to notify and how to initiate an internal investigation?

## Alarm Response

At 2:00 A.M. an alarm is received at the security console. The alarm panel indicates that an intrusion detection alarm on one of the exterior fire exits has been activated.

1. Did the console operator dispatch a security officer to investigate?
2. Did the console operator consider sending two security officers for added safety?
3. Did the console operator conduct a brief radio check to ensure that the security officers' radios were working properly?
4. Were the security officers equipped with flashlights?
5. Were the police notified?
6. Did the console operator lock down doors and elevators in the affected area to reduce access by the intruder(s)?

## Dealing with an Intoxicated Employee

While conducting a perimeter patrol at 9:30 P.M., a security officer encounters a man in business attire urinating against the side of the building. The security officer approaches the man and asks him to provide identification. The man turns and aggressively approaches the security officer. It is immediately apparent that he is very intoxicated, and as the man comes closer the security officer can smell the alcohol on his breath. The man starts berating the security officer for "bothering" him. The man waves his finger only inches from the security officer's face. He tells the security officer his name in a loud voice. He then states he is a senior vice president in the company and will have the security officer fired.

1. What action should the security officer take?
2. Who should be notified?
3. What paperwork should be generated?
4. What action should the security manager take in the aftermath of the incident?
5. In the aftermath of the incident, how can the security manager verify that the individual caught urinating is in fact who he claimed to be?

Clearly, an almost infinite number of hypothetical scenarios can be devised. Trainers should consider the types of incidents that have occurred at their facility and the type of incidents that would create the greatest problem using the probability/criticality model mentioned in Chapter 2.

## WALK THROUGH, TALK THROUGH EXERCISES

One application of the hypothetical situation is as a walk through, talk through exercise. As mentioned in Chapter 1, one variation of this exercise is referred to in the Marine Corps as a Tactical Evolution Without Troops (TEWT). The trainer chooses a security supervisor or security officer and presents him or her with a hypothetical scenario. The student must then walk the trainer through the facility and describe how he or she would assign other members of the security staff, where certain people and equipment would be located, what paths or routes would be used by whom, and so on. The following is an example of how a walk through, talk through exercise or TEWT might be conducted.

### Background

The location is in a chemical plant in an industrial park outside a major city. The security manager, Bill Smith, wants to train his weekend supervisor, John Jones, how to respond in the event of a hazardous material incident at the plant. Smith chooses to present

Jones with a hypothetical scenario and have Jones walk him through the steps he would take to respond. Smith, while conducting a weekend inspection of the plant, presents Jones with a scenario:

## Scenario

Due to a special request from a client, a shipment of a chemical compound is being packaged to be shipped on a Saturday afternoon. This is unusual, and a crew of drivers and distribution personnel have been called into the plant on short notice. Several members of the distribution crew and one of the drivers were known to have attended a party on Friday night. When they arrive at the plant they appear to be still suffering from the effects of the party. Due to the urgency of the shipment, the foreman does not worry about assessing their fitness to work. As several of the trucks are loaded, they begin to pull out of the cargo bays. There is a sudden, low-speed crash as one truck runs into the back of another truck outside the bays. The container of the first truck is broken open and the chemical begins to leak onto the ground. The foreman, aware that this chemical possesses dangerous properties, makes a frantic call to the security office. Smith asks Jones to lead him through the emergency response.

## Jones's Actions

Supervisor Jones indicates that he would have the console operator immediately notify the fire department and the plant management representative on call. He then leads Smith to where the Material Safety Data Sheets are located and turns to the page for the chemical in question. He explains how he would alert the security personnel on post to the spill. He then goes outside and indicates to Smith the area he would cordon off to isolate the spill and explains to whom he would delegate that responsibility. He then goes to the area where the first aid kit and decontamination equipment is located. He indicates the area where the drivers and other personnel who were in the vicinity of the spill would be taken, who would be responsible for leading them to safety, and what protective gear the security personnel would need when entering the spill area. He then shows Smith where he would post security watches to ensure that nobody accidentally entered the spill area. Jones then leads Smith to the main gate of the facility and explains that he would position a security officer near the main gate to escort emergency personnel to the spill area. He also explains that the escort would be equipped with a copy of the relevant page from the Material Safety Data Sheets to present to the fire chief. He explains to Smith the route the escort would use when leading the emergency personnel to the spill area. Jones finishes by explaining the reporting steps in the aftermath of the incident and the need for a possible investigation of the fitness for duty of the employees involved. Jones notes that a drug test is standard procedure following any accident of this sort.

### Smith's Critique

Security Manager Bill Smith is generally pleased with how Supervisor Jones described his proposed handling of the incident. He does question Jones on his ability to deploy so many people so quickly and suggests that Jones utilize several company messenger vehicles to make his force more mobile.

In this situation the security manager, Bill Smith, was able to see that the weekend supervisor, John Jones, was able to demonstrate how he would respond to a hazardous material incident at the plant. Jones was forced to consider how he would respond and to actually "walk the ground." In contrast with simply discussing the scenario in a classroom environment, Jones was able to get a feel for it. He had a greater appreciation of distances, routes that would have to be taken, and potential obstacles that he and his security team might encounter. It is doubtful that he would have had the same realization of these factors if he simply verbalized his response in the classroom. By discussing the situation with Smith he came to realize that by utilizing the company messenger vehicles, which sit unused on weekends, he could reduce the response time to the incident. Because only Smith and Jones were involved in the exercise, no security personnel needed to be taken off post to participate and not much coordination was required. Smith could include the training exercise as part of a regular inspection without disrupting the operations of the facility, spending hours planning and coordinating, and paying personnel to take part in the exercise.

There may be times when the trainer will want to involve several members of the security force without having a full-blown drill. In many cases the walk through, talk through mode can also be used to instruct the security personnel on their duties at a pace that would not be possible with a full drill. Using the same format as the example with Smith and Jones at the chemical plant, we can use the following example of an exercise incorporating several members of the staff.

## Background

A 25-story office building is in the downtown part of a major city. The building serves as the headquarters for XYZ corporation. Joe Williams is the director of security for XYZ, and Pete Harris is the security manager. Williams wants to be sure that the evening shift is able to respond effectively to medical emergencies, particularly because the company infirmary is closed and the nurse goes off duty at 5:30 P.M. Williams requests that Harris begin training and testing all off-hour shift personnel in medical emergency response. He is particularly concerned because there are several new people on these shifts with no practical experience dealing with medical emergencies at the building. Harris decides to begin the training with the evening shift. He chooses a walk through, talk through exercise to ensure that everyone has a clear understanding of the procedures and their individual duties.

## Scenario

There are five people assigned to the evening shift at the building: the supervisor, Mike Simmons, the console operator, and three security officers who rotate access-control and patrol responsibilities. The console has just received a call that an employee on the eighteenth floor is suffering from chest pains.

### Harris's Actions

Unlike in the previous scenario, Harris does not present the supervisor, Mike Simmons, with a problem to solve. Instead he explains to Simmons and the other members of the shift that at this point the console operator would gather as much information about the sick person as possible and call for an ambulance. He directs the console operator to remotely place an elevator on standby. He then leads Simmons and the three security officers and shows them where the escort for the ambulance crew will be placed. He explains the route the escort will use to the designated elevator. He leads Simmons and another security officer to the eighteenth floor and describes how that security officer should be assigned to wait with the victim, gather information, and ensure continued safety. As XYZ security personnel are certified in first aid and CPR, he discusses with Simmons and the security officer situations where the security officer may need to provide basic cardiac life support to the victim while awaiting the arrival of the ambulance. Harris then demonstrates how the security officer will escort the paramedics and the victim off the floor and out of the building. He finally discusses the report writing and documentation process as well as notification of security department management personnel. Throughout this process, Harris has walked the ground with Simmons and the security officers, explaining exactly what is expected of them.

### Reinforcement Drill

To ensure that everyone understands the procedures, Harris gives Simmons the same scenario and asks him to execute the proper response. At this point, Harris stands back and observes as Simmons walks his shift through the procedures, placing them in the proper positions and explaining each of the steps. Confident that Simmons and the members of his shift understand the procedures, Harris terminates the exercise. In two weeks the shift will conduct a full-speed drill to demonstrate that they are capable of performing the required tasks in a timely manner.

In the second example of a walk through, talk through exercise, the security manager led the members of the shift through a step-by-step explanation of the proper way to respond to a medical emergency at XYZ Corporation. By actually walking through the response, the security personnel were able to more clearly understand their responsibilities and the responsibilities of their team mates. After ensuring that the tasks were understood by all, the security manager directed the supervisor to carry out the exercise a second time. In many respects, this is similar to the chemical plant scenario, but in this case the supervisor is actually directing the security personnel. This also provides an opportunity to detect any problems or vagaries that may exist. These walk through, talk through exercises are the building blocks that prepare the security team for a full-speed drill. The drill, which is discussed in the next chapter, is probably the closest the security force will come to experiencing reality, short of an actual incident.

# 6

# *Emergency Drills: Putting Procedures into Practice*

In previous chapters we have discussed identifying the training needs that exist, using a procedures manual as a training aid, and using hypothetical and case studies in training. All of these elements form a foundation for the next stage of training: the drill. Drills provide the security manager with an opportunity to put the security force through a realistic simulation of an emergency or crisis situation. Drills will create a more realistic environment for the security force and will give security management a better appreciation of their capabilities than classroom hypothetical problem solving or walk through, talk through exercises. Drills do, however, require more planning, coordination and, in many cases, expense. It is frequently more beneficial to begin by running security force members through the type of training mentioned earlier to build a foundation. When the security staff has a clear understanding of their duties, a drill can be introduced to allow them to exhibit their skills under realistic conditions. Later, the security manager may wish to intersperse several drills with regular practical training such as hypothetical problem solving.

The goal of the drill should be to simulate as closely as possible the conditions of a real world situation. The trainees need to recognize that when real problems arise, things rarely go as smoothly as during conventional training. The instructor should make every effort to introduce realistic friction into the scenario. The term *friction* means difficulty. Friction is sometimes referred to as the *fog of war,* the stress, confusion, and uncertainty that are almost inevitable in a real-world crisis or emergency situation.

This is not to say that the instructor should confront the trainees with so many variables that the problem becomes unsolvable. The friction should be reasonable and of the type that realistically could be expected to occur. Likewise, friction should only be introduced into training after the security staff has demonstrated that they understand and are able to carry out their duties in a no-stress or low-stress environment. It is very important to adhere to this building block concept. The old adage that one must be able to crawl before they can walk and walk before they can run, definitely applies here. To introduce friction too early in training or to introduce it to such a degree that the situation becomes impossible can be very counterproductive. In these situations, the trainees may feel that they are facing an insurmountable task and that they are not properly trained or skilled to do their job. Introducing friction at the proper time, when the security staff has demonstrated a level of competency, can be incredibly valuable. In these situations, the members of the security force will realize that while things may not go as planned and Murphy's Law may come into play, they are sufficiently well trained to carry out the necessary tasks and adapt to the situation. The result will be security personnel who will respond more effectively in the face of a crisis situation.

How realistic the drill will be is dependent upon many factors, including budget, company philosophy, type of facility, and safety considerations. As stated in the introduction, many companies consider security to be a necessary evil and do not wish to expend time and effort or affect operations in order to ensure that they have a capable security force. Concerns about damage to property or personal injury are also factors. Frequently, realism must be compromised in order to ensure that the training is conducted safely. The objective of the security manager or trainer is to make the drill as realistic as possible within these constraints. The security manager must first assess these factors before planning the drill. As soon as the limitations and restrictions have been identified, the drill may be organized and conducted.

**Planning the drill** is a critical step. If proper time and effort is not expended up front to ensure quality training, it will almost always fall short of the desired result. Worse, it may serve to convince members of the security staff or the company at large that such exercises are pointless and a waste of time. The following are some factors that should be considered when planning a drill:

1. *Timing:* In most cases the drill should be scheduled for a time when it will have the least disruptive effect upon the operations of the organization. Weekends and other nonworking times are usually best. Often the focus of the drill will be the training of off-hour personnel who need to respond quickly when little supervision may be available. It is also necessary to train for responses that may occur during working hours when the facility is full of employees. Two notable incidents in New York City, the World Trade Center bombing and the Empire State Building shooting spree, both occurred during working hours when thousands of employees and visitors were in the buildings. Generally speaking, the only type of drills where all employees are involved is fire drills, and this is because they are usually mandated by local laws. The security manager can consider using several members of the security staff who are otherwise not involved in the drill to participate by playing the role of employees or visitors.

2. *Personnel:* Whenever possible, training should be conducted with the unit that works together. Conducting a drill involving members of the same shift working together will improve their teamwork and enhance their ability to respond as a unit. As mentioned above, some members of the security staff can play other roles in the drill. Another consideration should be the use of evaluators or assistant instructors in conducting the drill. In many cases these evaluators will be drawn from the security

staff. The topic of evaluators and assistant instructors will be covered more extensively later. If they are to be drawn from the staff, the security manager will have to determine who should be given this task and brief them on their duties.

3. *Equipment:* In some cases the only equipment that will be used is what is normally found on post: flashlights, portable radios, fire extinguishers, and so on. Other cases may involve more elaborate equipment like pyrotechnics or video equipment. This will be determined by the type of drill, the budget and the type of facility.

4. *Budget:* Even if no special equipment is involved, the drill can become expensive due to personnel costs. Since most line security personnel are hourly employees, they must be paid for participating in the drill. In many cases this will be in addition to their normal duties and will result in overtime. As a result, the drill should be scheduled to incur as little overtime as possible.

5. *Scenario:* The scenario for the drill can be drawn from a hypothetical situation or a case study, as discussed earlier.

6. *Objectives:* The security manager should determine in advance the goals that should be accomplished. These can be broad goals like: "Ensure that the security force can effectively respond to a medical emergency" or specific goals like: "Demonstrate the use of the elevator recall system."

7. *Evaluation:* How should the performance of the security staff during the drill be evaluated? Checklists and other guidelines can be used by the evaluators or assistant instructors. A debrief/critique session involving every person who took part in the drill is recommended when the exercise is over. This will allow the participants to identify and discuss some of the positive and negative aspects of the drill. This will not only cover the performance of the security staff in responding to the scenario, it will discuss the value of the drill as a whole. This will assist the security trainer in identifying problem areas regarding the organization and conduct of the drill and improving on future training exercises.

Once the security manager has determined these criteria, it will be easier to begin to plan the drill. One critical area which was mentioned earlier with regard to personnel, is the use of assistant instructors and evaluators. Unless the staff involved in the drill is very small, two or three people, and the entire staff will be in the same location, it will probably be necessary to have assistance in running the drill. The evaluators can be people drawn from the security staff. They should be chosen for their maturity and professionalism. In most cases, the security manager will want to develop an evaluation checklist that will assist the evaluator in monitoring the exercise. The checklist should be designed to ensure that the personnel involved in the drill are graded upon criteria the security manager has established. If the drill requires that the security force be split into several groups working in different parts of the facility, then an evaluator should accompany each group. Ideally, the evaluator will have a checklist designed for that particular group. The evaluators should understand the objectives of the training exercise and how it is to be accomplished. The instructor should meet with the evaluators, either individually or as a group, prior to the drill to discuss the goals and methods to be used during the exercise. Although the evaluators will be equipped with a checklist that will describe the tasks that should be accomplished by the trainees, they should also have sufficient experience to make objective observations and comments about the trainees' performance. Ideally, they will have experience in the very skill or task being drilled and will be able to detect areas for improvement. The evaluators will also have a key role in the critique phase as they can give an objective firsthand account of the security force's actions during the drill.

These concepts can be best understood by reviewing several sample drills. It is important to remember that the procedures described in these drills are used for illustrative purposes only and are not applicable for every organization or location. The goal is to use the example drills as a format to apply to your organization. For simplicity, all the sample drills are set at the fictitious XYZ Corporation headquarters. As you will recall, XYZ Corporation is based in a 25-story building in the business district of a major city.

## MEDICAL EMERGENCY

This drill will simulate the response to a medical emergency that occurs at XYZ Corporation during normal working hours. Different procedures will be drilled for an emergency occurring during evenings, nights, or weekends.

### Scenario

The security console receives a call from Janet Johnson, a company employee on the tenth floor. She tells the console operator that her boss, Harvey Wilson, is feeling pain and pressure in his chest and in his left arm.

### Response

The console operator should do the following:

1. Alert the company nurse to the situation and direct her to the tenth floor.

---

Medical Emergency Response Brief Sheet

Scenario: During an off-hours shift, a security officer is patrolling a lower level of the building. The security officer discovers a person unconscious on the floor in one of the hallways. (The victim will be simulated by a role player).

1. The security officer will respond to the victim.

2. The security officer will notify the shift supervisor.

3. The supervisor will coordinate the response measures

4. The evaluator will terminate the exercise when (a) appropriate action has been taken or (b)

    The designated time has elapsed.

Designated time: 30 minutes

**Figure 6–1.** Medical Emergency Response Brief Sheet

<u>Medical Emergency – Evaluator Checklist</u>

| | | |
|---|---|---|
| 1. Did the security officer attempt to make the victim? | Yes | No |
| 2. Did the security officer attempt to move the victim? | Yes | No |
| 3. Did the security officer check airway-breathing-circulation? | Yes | No |
| 4. Did the security officer notify the supervisor? | Yes | No |
| 5. Did the supervisor make proper notifications? | Yes | No |
| 6. Did the supervisor attempt to protect the victim from further harm? | Yes | No |
| 7. Did the supervisor have an elevator standing by? | Yes | No |
| 8. Did the supervisor send an escort to meet the EMTs? | Yes | No |
| 9. Did the supervisor get the necessary information for a report? | Yes | No |
| 10. Was the report completed properly? | Yes | No |

Comments:_____

_____

_____

_____

_____

_____

_____

Supervisor:_____     Evaluator:_____

S/O 1:_____     Date:_____

S/O 2:_____     Time:_____

S/O 3:_____

**Figure 4-1.** Medical Emergency Evaluator Checklist

2. Dispatch a security officer to the tenth floor to assist the victim and conduct crowd control if necessary.
3. Contact Emergency Medical Service and request an ambulance. Give the dispatcher all the information from the initial call from Janet Johnson regarding Harry Wilson, including his age, any prescription or nonprescription drugs he may be taking, prior medical conditions, and his symptoms if this information was learned.
4. Contact company security director and shift supervisor to make them aware of the situation.
5. Notify security officer at the main gate to expect the ambulance and to direct them to the main entrance.
6. Dispatch a security officer to the main entrance to escort ambulance crew.
7. Direct freight elevator to be on standby in the lobby.

The shift supervisor should do the following:

1. Verify that the dispatched security officers are reporting to their assigned positions.
2. Verify that the freight elevator is on standby in the lobby.
3. Prepare to make liaison with the ambulance crew.

The security staff should then make contact with the role-players representing the ambulance crew for the purpose of the drill. They will then escort them to the tenth floor, where a role-player representing the victim will be located. The actions of the ambulance crew will not be simulated (unless the ambulance crew are part of the company staff and are involved in the drill to train their skills as well). The ambulance crew will then be escorted from the facility by the security staff members.

## Post-incident Activity

At this point in the drill, the coordinator will assign a report-writing exercise for those personnel who would have to generate an incident report.

## Critique

After the exercise the instructor should gather all the participants, including any role-players, in a quiet area. The drill should then be reviewed phase by phase to identify both positive and negative aspects. The scenario should be repeated for all present. Many times personnel, especially those on the periphery, such as the security officer at the main gate, may not know the full scenario. This review will allow everyone to better appreciate the comments and observations that are made. Next the instructor should lead a discussion of each stage of the response. Participants can make both positive and negative observations about their own and others' actions. This should be done in a professional, constructive way. The instructor should act as a moderator to ensure that the discussion remains on track. Role-players often have valuable insight into the actions of participants and should be solicited for comments and opinions. The instructor should review the reports that were generated and discuss how, if at all, they can be improved. Finally, the participants should be encouraged to discuss the drill and its premise and to offer opinions on how to improve future exercises.

## BOMB THREAT

This drill will simulate the response to a telephone bomb threat.

### Scenario

A call is received by the security officer posted at the main lobby reception desk. The caller makes the following statement: "I have planted a bomb in the building, and it will explode in one hour!"

### Response

The security officer answering the call should do the following:

1. Stay on the line to gather as much information as possible from the caller.

2. Copy the caller's exact words.
3. Lift a red file folder in the air to alert the lobby access-control officer that a bomb threat is being received.
4. Begin completing the bomb threat checklist.
   a. When is the bomb going to explode?
   b. Where is the bomb right now?
   c. What does the bomb look like?
   d. What kind of bomb is it?
   e. What will cause the bomb to explode?
   f. Did you place the bomb?
   g. Why?
   h. What is your address?
   I. What is your name?
5. Hang up only after the caller hangs up.

The lobby access-control officer should do the following upon seeing the red file folder:

1. Notify the shift supervisor and console operator in the security console by telephone.
2. Maintain control of general lobby operations so the reception desk officer can deal with the threat phone call without interruption.

Upon notification, the supervisor and console operator should do the following:

1. Notify the police.
2. Notify the security director and security manager.
3. Activate the bomb threat plan.

Assuming that XYZ Corporation procedures include conducting a building search while awaiting the arrival of the police, a drill could commence regarding the bomb search. This bomb search drill could be done in conjunction with the bomb threat drill or separately. If the bomb search drill was being done separately or not at all, the instructor could proceed to the post-incident phase.

### Post-incident Phase

The personnel involved will write reports describing the incident. The person receiving the call will complete any unfinished parts of the bomb threat checklist.

### Critique

The instructor may wish to record the threat phone call and play it back to review the following criteria:

1. How accurate was the description on the bomb threat checklist of the caller's voice?
2. Were any background noises present? Were they recorded accurately on the bomb threat checklist?
3. Were the caller's words copied exactly?
4. Were the right questions asked and was everything done to get as much information as possible?

The instructor may also wish to review each report for clarity and consistency and review with each participant his or her role in the drill.

## BOMB SEARCH

This drill can be done in conjunction with the bomb threat drill, subsequent to the bomb threat drill, or entirely separately.

### Scenario

Assuming this is a continuation of the bomb threat drill: The call has been received and notifications made. XYZ procedures call for a search of the facility by members of the security force (some companies use fire wardens or other company employees, but XYZ prefers to use only building staff).

### Response

The supervisor's response should be:

1. Designate searchers/search teams.
2. Designate areas of responsibility.
3. Implement alternate communication plan (XYZ company procedures call for no use of radio equipment during bomb threats or bomb incidents due to the possibility of initiating an electrical firing system/electric blasting cap. Many companies differ on this policy and some law enforcement agencies recommend using radios up to the point where a suspect item is found). Primary communication will be made by conventional telephone, secondary communication by messenger.
4. Briefly review with searchers what their actions should be when encountering a suspect item.

   The searchers actions should include:

1. Focusing first on public access areas:
   a. The exterior of the building
   b. The lobby
   c. Trashcans and planters
   d. Stairwells
   e. Restrooms
2. While searching rooms, divide by height and search:
   a. Floor to waist
   b. Waist to head
   c. Head to ceiling
   d. Ceiling itself if it is a drop ceiling
3. Use marking to indicate rooms/areas already searched and cleared.
4. If a suspect item is found the searchers should take the following action:
   a. Do not touch it.
   b. Isolate the item (at least 300 feet; ATF is now advocating 1,000 feet and 1 to 3 floors above and below if the item is on an interior floor).

c. Use marking to designate isolation area.
d. Be aware of possible second device.
e. Make liaison with police upon their arrival.

## Post-incident Phase

Again, the personnel involved should write a report detailing the incident and the action taken. Procedures for re-entering the area after the threat has been removed may be discussed.

## Critique

The instructor should discuss each phase of the bomb search with the participants. Key points are:

1. Priority of search areas
2. Search techniques
3. Designation of sectors of responsibility
4. Actions upon encountering a suspect item
5. Consideration of a second device
6. Isolation of the suspect item area

# SUSPECT LETTER/PARCEL

This drill involves the screening of letters and packages by security personnel. The drill can be designed to incorporate the use of x-ray screening devices or general visual screening techniques by noting characteristics of the letter or parcel.

## Scenario

A member of the security staff assigned to the CEO's protection team is working on post on the executive floor. As part of his routine he visually inspects all deliveries from the mailroom to the CEO. Today, while he is checking the mail, he notices a box about the size of a videotape. The box is wrapped in brown paper and is addressed by hand to the CEO. The box was postmarked three days ago in

Manama, Bahrain, and there are numerous stamps affixed to the package. The package is also wrapped with heavy tape. On one side there are several moist stains. The box also seems unusually heavy and unbalanced for its size.

## Response

The security screener who noticed the problem should:

1. Place the package down and refrain from handling it any further.
2. Isolate the area around the package and mark it off.
3. Notify the security supervisor and console operator of the situation.

The security supervisor and console operator should do the following:

1. Notify the police.
2. Notify the security director/upper management.
3. Attempt to learn from the CEO's secretary if the package was expected.
4. If a return address is present, attempt to contact the sender to determine if the package is legitimate.
5. Ensure that a member of the security staff is available to make liaison with the police/bomb squad and escort them to the suspect item.

## Post-incident Phase

All key personnel should write reports of the incident.

## Critique

The instructor will review with the screener why the package was suspicious. The supervisor and console operator will describe the actions they took, including attempts to verify the legitimacy of the package.

## BUILDING EVACUATION

This drill will simulate procedures to be followed to evacuate part or all of the building due to an unsafe condition.

### Scenario

A fire in the sub-basement elevator motor room is causing smoke to travel up the elevator shafts in a "chimney" effect. It is determined that the building should be evacuated while firefighters extinguish the blaze. If the fire was occurring on an upper floor, the scenario could involve evacuating only the fire floors and two floors above. In most cases it would be preferable to begin by drilling the evacuation of several floors rather than using an entire building evacuation as the first drill.

### Response

The fire safety director should do the following:

1. Marshal the evacuation teams at the fire command center.
2. Make an all-call using the building public address system advising building occupants that there is a condition requiring the evacuation of the building. Request all floor wardens to assemble the employees on their respective floor by the exit and await further instructions.
3. Dispatch evacuation teams to their assigned areas to assist the evacuation.
4. Dividing the building into quarters, the Fire Safety Director will evacuate one floor per quarter simultaneously. This will prevent too many people from being in one stairwell at a time, will reduce the chance of injury, and will generally expedite the evacuation. The Fire Safety Director will use the PA system to call only the floors being evacuated at that particular time.
5. The Fire Safety Director will make periodic notifications over the all-call to reassure tenants awaiting evacuation that the situation is under control to reduce the possibility of panic.

The members of the evacuation teams should perform the following duties, depending on their specific team assignments. These assignments should be made prior to the actual drill.

1. Team members should be assigned to make liaison with fire department members responding to the emergency.
2. Team members should be assigned specifically to assist in the evacuation of disabled people. These members should be specially trained in emergency carries with special equipment such as Medi-Chair evacuation devices and expedient carries using standard chairs. Training managers should consider bringing in an outside instructor to conduct this training. Tenants with disabilities should be listed in the building fire plan and their locations should be known to evacuation team members.
3. Team members should be designated to link up with floor wardens and their tenant parties and direct them to pre-established rally points away from the building.

Employee floor wardens and searchers should take the following action:

1. Gather all floor personnel by the emergency exit on the floor.
2. Ensure that all floor occupants are present. Search restrooms and other areas to ensure that nobody is left behind. This is particularly true on floors where there may be many visitors or others not normally working on that particular floor.
3. Follow instructions as given by the Fire Safety Director over building public address system. Attempt to ensure that floor employees remain calm.
4. Upon the direction of the Fire Safety Director, lead the tenants of the floor into the stairwell and down to a safe area. In the case of this drill, which is a total building evacuation, lead floor employees into the lobby and, following the directions of evacuation team members, lead them to the rally point.
5. At the rally point, take attendance to ensure that all are present. Report any missing personnel to evacuation team members.

### Post-incident Phase

Evacuation team members can practice conducting an organized reentry of the building when a safe condition has been declared

### Critique

The instructor can review the various phases of the evacuation with evacuation team members, the Fire Safety Director and, if they took part in the drill, the floor wardens and searchers. Communication is a key factor in any evacuation. Were the Fire Safety Director's instructions clear over the PA system? Did floor wardens know their duties in advance? Did evacuation team members know where to report and what to do?

### Notes

Drills simulating an evacuation should be held in addition to the normal fire drills required by most municipalities. These drills should involve key players like the floor wardens if possible, but will generally not involve all building employees. The scope and depth of this operation make it too disruptive for most organizations to include their entire workforce. A good resource for evacuation planning and other building emergency response techniques is *High-Rise Security and Fire Life Safety* by Geoff Craighead, Butterworth–Heinemann, 1996. Additional information can be found by contacting a local fire department or the National Fire Protection Association.

## ELEVATOR ENTRAPMENT DRILL

This scenario depicts a fairly routine situation that occurs in multistory commercial office buildings like the one where XYZ Corporation is headquartered.

### Scenario

At 10 P.M. on a Wednesday night, the security officer posted in the building lobby receives an elevator alarm.

### Response

The security officer in the lobby should:

1. Contact the elevator's occupants through the intercom.
2. Determine the nature of the problem.
3. Upon learning that the elevator is stuck with three people inside, inform them that steps are being taken to free them and request that they remain calm.
4. Check the elevator system display and determine the location and status of the elevator car.
5. Notify the security console of the situation.
6. Ask the occupants for their names and departments. Ask the occupants if the security officer can assist them by making a courtesy phone call to anyone who may be waiting for them.
7. Maintain constant communication with the occupants throughout the entrapment to reduce the chance of panic. Determine if the occupants have any special needs or medical problems.

The console operator should take the following steps:

1. Notify an on-call elevator mechanic to respond.
2. Notify the shift supervisor.
3. Dispatch a security officer to the nearest floor to meet the occupants when the elevator is opened.
4. Dispatch a security officer to meet the mechanic upon arrival and escort him to the console to be briefed on the entrapment.

### Post-incident Phase

The security officer on the floor should meet the occupants when they are released and verify their identities and ensure that they are all safe and healthy. The personnel involved should prepare reports detailing the incident.

### Critique

The instructor should analyze how well the security staff was able to keep the passengers calm throughout the entrapment. While this is a relatively routine situation, it can rapidly become a serious emergency. The instructor could add friction by using a role-player as one of the people trapped in the elevator to simulate a victim with claustrophobia who begins to panic.

## RIOT/CIVIL DISTURBANCE

This drill could be used to simulate a situation where there is a period of civil unrest in the vicinity of the organization's facility. Even if the action is not directed at the company itself, the mere fact that it is occurring in close proximity to the company's facility creates a dangerous situation. While this is a relatively rare occurrence in the United States, there are several situations that come to mind where commercial facilities were threatened by civil unrest situations. The Los Angeles riots of 1992 are perhaps the most extreme example in recent history. During this period there was a temporary breakdown in law and order and public authorities were unable to maintain control of the violence in the streets. The violent West Virginia coal mining strikes of the 1980s were a different, but also very threatening type of situation. Even relatively benign situations such as fans celebrating their team's championship win have gotten out of control and resulted in damage to property. Companies with international operations should definitely consider these types of drills for their overseas facilities, particularly those in unstable areas of the world.

### Scenario

A group of activists has gathered outside XYZ corporate headquarters to protest XYZ's dealings with a foreign country alleged to be responsible for many human rights abuses. What was expected to be a relatively small protest involving several student groups has turned out to be a much larger group including many members of hard-line radical groups that espouse violence. The police assigned to the demonstration, not anticipating such a large crowd are having difficulty controlling it.

### Response

The shift supervisor, upon noticing the size and agitation of the crowd, should take the following action:

1. Immediately notify the director of security.
2. Direct security staff to close all nonessential entrances to the facility and concentrate additional security personnel at the main entrance.
3. Dispatch two security officers to an upper floor to watch the crowd from the window and report their activities to the security console.

The security console operator should take the following action:

1. Limit the number of security personnel on meal break. Keep those on break in a stand-by mode, accessible by radio.
2. Notify building occupants of the situation outside and recommend they remain within the facility until the situation is under control.

### Post-incident Phase

The supervisor, console operator, and designated security personnel should complete reports detailing the incident. The incident should not be considered resolved until additional police have arrived and dispersed the crowd.

### Critique

The instructor should review the speed and effectiveness of communication and response to securing entrances/exits, and so on. The observations of the security officers posted on the upper floor should be reviewed.

### Note

Unless the trainer can get a large crowd of role-players to play the demonstrators (which is unlikely and may cause a real public safety problem if they are mistaken by police for the real thing) some aspects of this drill will have to be constructive. Security officers will have to be told what the "crowd" is doing and will have to use some imagination.

## WORKPLACE VIOLENCE INVOLVING A WEAPON

This drill simulates the response by security to an incident of workplace violence when a weapon is involved or believed to be involved.

### Scenario

A recently terminated employee has returned to the building to remove personal property. A representative from the human resources department escorts him to his former workspace. Human resources declined the offer of a security escort because they fear the presence of a security officer will only anger and upset the man and create a tense situation. Things are proceeding smoothly until the man's former supervisor passes by the workspace. Words are exchanged and the terminated employee lunges at the supervisor. A quick flurry of blows occurs and the supervisor falls backwards to the floor. Initially the other employees think that the supervisor has been punched and they rush forward to break up the fight. Blood soon covers the supervisor's shirt and the employees notice a folding knife in the hand of the terminated employee. Realizing that the supervisor has been stabbed and that the assailant is still armed, the employees who came forward to break up the fight begin backing away. The supervisor is rapidly losing blood and going into shock. The former employee slashes the human resources representative in the arm. The cut is relatively superficial, but the victim is panicked and begins screaming. One of the employees on the floor reaches a phone and calls the security office.

## Response

The console operator receives the call and takes the following action:

1. Calls 911 and requests police and medical assistance
2. Notifies the lobby security personnel to dispatch a security officer to the street in front of the building to make liaison with the police and escort them to the floor
3. Places an elevator on manual service and dispatches a security officer to operate the elevator for police and emergency medical personnel
4. Notifies the shift supervisor and management of the situation and the steps that have been taken thus far

The shift supervisor should do the following:

1. Report to the lobby and ensure that all security personnel are posted properly.
2. Make liaison with the police upon their arrival and inform them that the assailant is still on the floor and armed.
3. Ensure that all information is gathered for post-incident documentation.

## Post-incident Phase

All involved parties should complete incident report documentation describing the incident and security's response.

## Critique

The following questions could be asked of the participants during a critique:

1. Did security respond quickly and fluidly?
2. Would an attempt to isolate the floor to contain the situation have further endangered the employees on the floor by trapping them?

3. Could security officers have responded to the injured employees without endangering themselves?

4 Could security have prevented additional employees from entering the danger area without simultaneously trapping other employees on the floor?

5. Should other employees in the building be notified when the incident is occurring? If so, how?

6. Would the incident be handled differently if the former had punched the supervisor and not stabbed him and if no weapon appeared? If so, how?

## CRITIQUING DRILLS

Critiquing drills when they are completed can be a valuable tool for improving security readiness. A key element of the critique is to establish objectives in advance. The evaluator checklists mentioned earlier, can be used to spell out specific objectives for each part and phase of the drill. One effective method for conducting a critique is for the instructor to gather all the participants in the drill-trainees, evaluators, and so on—and review each phase of the drill step by step. After the instructor introduces a portion of the drill and recalls the sequence of events in that phase, each evaluator can discuss his or her observations. The participants will then get an opportunity to make comments or ask questions. The instructor will then summarize and move on to the next phase of the drill, where the process will be repeated.

As mentioned previously, critiques should be conducted in the spirit of constructive criticism. Both positive and negative points should be highlighted and discussed. When the critique is complete, the trainee should recognize areas where both he or she and the group need to improve. Ideally, the trainee should also come away from the drill and critique with a renewed feeling of confidence and recognize that serious situations can be managed and controlled effectively, if not perfectly, and that a successful resolution is achievable.

## IMMEDIATE ACTION DRILLS

Another useful training device is the immediate action drill. Unlike the more elaborate drills described earlier in this chapter, immediate action drills are simply repetitions of prearranged responses to given situations. Therefore, the security person knows that if "A happens, I do B." This method, taken from the military, designates specific responses to anticipated security threats. When the threat occurs, each member of the security team has practiced his or her role and knows exactly what to do.

In military units, immediate action drills are practiced by small units to prepare them to respond to possible threats. For example, if a squad is assigned to undertake a security patrol to determine if there is any enemy activity in the area near the larger unit's position, the squad will normally rehearse prior to the operation. Part of this rehearsal will involve immediate action drills. Before going on the patrol, the squad will practice different situations. If there is enemy contact to the front, designated members will return fire while the others withdraw to a position where they will begin firing to allow the first team to withdraw. Using this method the squad can "leapfrog" to safety, covering each other's withdrawal. Similar actions are taken if there is an ambush on either flank. During the rehearsals, the squad repeats the drills numerous times until each person understands his or her role in relation to the others.

These techniques are very adaptable to the security practitioner. Security personnel face a number of foreseeable threats and emergency situations. Immediate action drills can be developed for most of these incidents. If these drills are practiced on a regular basis, they will greatly increase the chance of a successful resolution when a situation occurs.

Immediate action drills, once they are developed, can be practiced on a weekly, even daily basis. The person generally responsible for the conduct of the immediate action drill will be the shift supervisor. The drill usually will have been devised in conjunction with the trainer or security manager, but it can be practiced on the lowest level. Immediate action drills are one of the few practical training techniques where critiques are not normally conducted after each drill.

Consider the following example of an immediate action drill for responding to a medical emergency. For purposes of the drill there is a console operator, designated C/O and five security officers numbered one through five.

The shift supervisor calls the security console on an internal phone line and prefaces the conversation with the phrase "immediate action drill" so there is no confusion that this is a drill. He then tells the console operator that the scenario is that a 50-year-old, male employee is suffering from chest pains on the sixth floor, east side. The console operator notifies the staff that it is an immediate action drill and then says, "Medical emergency, sixth floor east, male, chest pains."

1. The C/O then calls 911 (simulated).
2. Officers #1 and #2 take the elevator to the sixth floor east to locate the victim and give first aid if necessary.
3. Officer #3 places the elevator on manual service and stands by to operate it.
4. Officer #4 goes outside the front entrance to serve as an escort for the ambulance crew.
5. Officer #5 remains on post in the front lobby, enforcing the access-control policy.

The supervisor, after viewing the staff conduct the drill correctly, notifies the console operator to terminate the drill. The staff members all return to their respective posts.

The immediate action drill took only several minutes and caused no disruption in the normal routine. Each member went straight to his or her designated task with a minimum of direction from the console operator. This happened quickly without the need for the console operator to say, "Smith go here, Jones go there . . ." and without the confusion of two people performing the same task while another job went undone. When a real situation arises, the shift members should know what is expected of them and respond quickly. This drill is an excellent tool during off-hours shifts but is also generally unobtrusive enough to be conducted during weekday shifts at nonpeak times. While the immediate action drill does not accomplish all the goals or give the realistic feel of a full-blown emergency response drill, it makes up for many of those deficiencies by being economical and easy to practice. As a result, it can be conducted frequently and can greatly improve the performance of the security staff and enhance their ability to work as a team.

Conducting a regular routine of immediate action drills in conjunction with periodic emergency response drills will greatly enhance the ability of the security force to respond to emergencies. The constant practice and increased familiarization will not only make the security officers more knowledgeable about emergency response, it will also significantly increase their confidence.

## REFERENCE

Craighead, Geoff. *High-Rise Security and Fire Life Safety.* Boston: Butterworth–Heinemann, 1996.

# 7

# Role-Play: Getting a Feel for "Real-Life" Situations

Human relations play a major role in security work. Effective security personnel need to be able to deal with a wide variety of types of people to be successful. These interpersonal dealings take place during routine activities and also during emergency situations. Role-play can be a very effective vehicle for training in both types of situations. There are many types of emergency drills that can encompass role-playing, particularly when the instructor wants to introduce friction into the scenario. For example, during an evacuation drill, the instructor can designate a role-player to simulate a building employee who insists on reentering the building to retrieve some personal item. The security personnel must deal with this added problem of the insistent employee attempting to reenter a hazardous area while still conducting the evacuation in an efficient, orderly manner.

The following examples, taken from the military, illustrate how role-play can be introduced into a larger training exercise to add realism, friction, and uncertainty. These examples are typical of the types of difficult missions the military trains for in the modern, post–Cold War world. These drills are also particularly instructive because they bear some similarity to emergency situations security forces may face.

## EXAMPLES FROM THE MILITARY

### *Noncombatant Evacuation*

The noncombatant evacuation operation, or NEO, is an example of what the military calls Operations Other Than War (OOTW). Since 1975, the U.S. military has conducted these operations in Vietnam, Cambodia, Liberia, Haiti, Somalia, and Albania to name a few. Many of the characteristics of these operations are similar to evacuations security professionals may have to conduct under emergency conditions.

### Scenario

Political instability in a foreign country has forced the United States to evacuate diplomatic personnel and other American citizens. A battalion of Marines is tasked with the evacuation. Landing by helicopter, one Marine rifle company reaches the American embassy, where most of the American citizens have gathered. After establishing perimeter security, they begin to process and move the Americans to a rally point to be evacuated by helicopter. Throughout this exercise, role-players simulating evacuees present additional challenges to the Marines. Some of the characters the role-players represent include:

1. A wealthy U.S. businessman who wants a squad of Marines to escort him back to his apartment to retrieve a piece of valuable artwork
2. A pregnant woman who begins going into labor
3. A foreign national, employed by the embassy, who demands to be evacuated
4. An arrogant diplomat who refuses to cooperate with the evacuation plan
5. An American family that insists on bringing their luggage and two dogs

### *Cordon and Search of a Village*

This training exercise reflects many of the challenges that the military has faced dealing with unconventional warfare. Security professionals may see some parallels to security situations where suspects are to be questioned in the aftermath of an incident.

### Scenario

This scenario involves a counterinsurgency situation in a third world country. The antigovernment guerillas hide among the civilian population, appearing only to strike and then vanish again. An infantry platoon is assigned to patrol a certain sector to locate signs of the guerilla force. The platoon approaches a local village. Two squads encircle the village to prevent anyone from entering or leaving. The third squad, along with the platoon commander and radio operator, enters the village to search for weapons and equipment, and to interview the inhabitants. Role-players act as the villagers. Some of the roles include:

1. A villager who becomes very upset at the troops, begins yelling at them and refuses to allow them to search his shack
2. A village chief who reports that a guerilla unit just left the village minutes earlier and offers to lead the platoon in pursuit, but insists they must go immediately, which will prevent the search of the village
3. A villager, apparently unarmed, who runs out of the village

How do these examples translate to a security environment? In each situation the role-players introduce a human element that complicates the scenario. This is a very important aspect of realistic training, because this is exactly the sort of thing that happens in real life. Dealing with different types of people, especially in the midst of a crisis situation, is the sort of thing for which security personnel must be prepared.

We will soon review some specific examples of role-play scenarios in the security arena. But first it is important to review and consider some of the problems and obstacles to role-play. Role play can be difficult for several reasons. First, who will be the role-players? While many participants in the drill will be involved in role-play, there are generally several antagonists who are not trainees participating in the drill but rather pure role-players whose sole duty is to confront the trainees with difficult situations. The role-players mentioned in the two military exercises above are examples of role-player antagonists. The first and most obvious answer is to use members of the security force who are not participating as trainees to fill these positions. The problem: Play acting in front of a group does not come naturally to many, if not most, adults. Additionally, when many of the members of the security force work together and know each other well, it may be difficult for them to treat the exercise seriously. Can outsiders be used as role-players? In some cases, yes. If the organization is situated in an area where there are colleges, the instructor can consider making contact with the drama department. Drama students may be willing to assist the company's training exercise through role-playing for academic credit or simply experience. Before bringing students or other outsiders into the facility to assist with training, however, the instructor should get approval from company management. Liability concerns should be examined; for example, what if a role-player is injured during the exercise? If approval is granted to bring the outside role-players to take part in the exercise, use of release forms is advisable.

In many cases outside role-players will not be a viable option. If the role-players are drawn from the security staff, the trainer should consider using personnel who are extroverted and have a personality that lends itself to performance. While the trainees will also be involved in role-playing, the antagonist role-players, mentioned earlier, will need to be strong enough to guide the scenario.

In some situations the trainer may also wish to use team role-play. The American Management Association's *Trainer's Handbook* (see Chapter 1) recommends using team role-play to help overcome problems of shyness, stage fright, and general reluctance to participate. This type of training is better suited to a classroom environment than to an on-site practical training exercise. In this exercise, the trainer divides the class into groups or teams and presents a scenario. Each team is then assigned a role within the scenario. The teams meet privately to discuss a strategy for acting out the scenario. The teams then either choose a role-player to represent them or, if the group is small enough, each member takes a turn as the role-player. The class reconvenes and the teams take turns acting out the scenario. This environment is generally considered more supportive and less threatening by the participants.

While much of our discussion has focused on the introduction of role-play into emergency response training, it is important to remember that it can be utilized as effectively for training in everyday situations. With the increased need for good customer service and public relations skills by security personnel, role-play can be an excellent tool to develop and eventually test these skills. The following sample role-play situations encompass both routine situations and emergency response situations.

## EXAMPLES FROM BUSINESS

### *Non-English–Speaking Visitor Who Is Violating Company Policies*

A security officer making a routine patrol at XYZ Corporation observes a middle-aged man attempting to enter through a fire exit door that has been propped open. The security officer approaches the man and informs him that he must go to the visitors' reception desk to obtain authorization to enter the building and to receive a pass. The man responds to the security officer by speaking in a foreign language the security officer does not recognize and continuing to walk through the door.

### Role-play Exercise

The security officer must attempt to communicate to the man that he cannot enter through the fire exit. He must do this tactfully and in a nonthreatening manner, but must also communicate firmly despite the language barrier. The role-player simulating the foreign language–speaking man must persist in attempting to enter the building and must communicate only in a foreign language to the security officer. When and if the security officer is able to effectively communicate his point, the role player will stop trying to enter the door and will accompany the security officer to the reception desk and the exercise will cease.

## Dealing with an Angry Customer Who Refuses to Leave

The security officer assigned to the lobby reception area is approached by a man claiming to be a customer of XYZ Corporation. The man tells the security officer he wants to see someone in the sales department to make a complaint. When the security officer asks him for a contact name in the sales department he refuses to give one and becomes upset. The security officer places a phone call to the receptionist in the sales department and explains the situation. The receptionist informs the security officer that the man cannot be admitted without an appointment and recommends that he call the sales department from home and schedule an appointment for another day. When the security officer informs the visitor of this he becomes irate and begins yelling in the building lobby. The visitor insists he is going to remain in the building lobby until he is seen by someone in sales and that nothing else will persuade him to leave.

### Role-play Exercise

The security officer must attempt to calm the man down because his yelling is creating a disturbance in the building lobby. The security officer may additionally call for a supervisor, who can then join in the scenario. The second concern is convincing the man to leave the building and schedule an appointment at a future time. The role-player simulating the visitor should steadfastly refuse to leave the building until his complaints have been heard by someone in sales. He should threaten to remain at the reception desk all night if necessary. He can vacillate between being relatively calm and having sudden loud outbursts of yelling.

## Person Removing Property Without Authorization

A security officer posted in the building lobby during an evening shift at XYZ headquarters observes a woman carrying a large box stepping from the elevator and walking toward the exit. It is XYZ company policy for anyone removing property from the building to have a property pass describing the items being removed and signed by an authorized signatory. As the woman approaches, the security officer asks her for the property pass. The woman replies that she doesn't have a pass and that she is in a hurry. The security officer explains the corporate policy regarding property removal and requests that the woman return upstairs for a pass. The woman tells the security officer that everyone with authorized signatory status in her department has left for the day and that the materials in the box are needed for a presentation the next day at an out-of-town client's office.

**Role-play Exercise**

The security officer must attempt to get authorization for the employee to remove the box and must convince the employee to wait while authorization is granted or the security officer must direct the employee to leave the materials in the building. The role-player representing the employee with the box must persist in trying to leave with the materials. The role-player must repeatedly explain that it is vital that the materials are available for the presentation. The role-player must also make reference to being in a hurry, needing to catch a train, and become angry at being detained by the security officer.

## *Assessing an Injury Victim*

A security officer at XYZ is dispatched by the console operator to respond to a report of an injured employee on the tenth floor. Upon arriving on the tenth floor the security officer finds a group of employees gathered around a person lying on the floor. The person is conscious and complaining of head and back pain.

**Role-play Exercise**

The security officer must be concerned with obtaining the names and extensions of possible witnesses and then dispersing the crowd. The security officer must also notify the console to contact emergency medical service personnel and must begin to gather vital information about the victim and how the injuries were sustained. The role-player representing the victim can play the role as dazed, in shock, panicked, or in any other manner that will force the trainee to react. Additional role-players can represent the employees on the floor who gather around the victim, provide conflicting information, or attempt to move the victim. The trainee will then have to effectively deal with these situations, as well.

## Elevator Entrapment with a Panicked Occupant

The security officer assigned to the front lobby receives an elevator alarm. Upon making contact with the occupants, the security officer determines that the elevator is stuck between floors. While the security console operator makes contact with an elevator mechanic to resolve the problem, the lobby security officer uses the intercom to communicate with the occupants of the elevator. There is one person within the elevator. This person becomes very panicked and tells the security officer that due to a problem with claustrophobia, the person cannot remain in the elevator.

### Role-play Exercise

The security officer must attempt to calm the person down while awaiting help. The role-player representing the entrapped person must continually panic, yell at the security officer through the intercom, and threaten to open the roof hatch and climb out of the elevator into the shaftway.

## Employee Termination

Security is called to be present at the termination of an employee for cause. A security officer is dispatched to sit outside the office in the human resources department where the termination is taking place. Following the termination, the security officer is to accompany the former employee and supervisor to clean out the former employees office. The security officer is then to escort the person from the building.

**Role-play Exercise**

The role-player representing the terminated employee may act out during the actual termination, requiring the security officer to intervene. During the removal of the terminated employee's belongings, the role-player may attempt to remove company property. The role-player may also delay when being escorted out of the building and claim to want to say goodbye to coworkers.

Clearly there is an almost limitless number of situations, from critical to relatively mundane, that can be role played. As with the case studies and hypothetical scenarios discussed earlier in the book, the trainer can gather material for the scenarios from events that have occurred at the facility or similar facilities.

Critiques of role-play situations should follow a similar format to the critiques outlined earlier in this book. When the role-play is part of a larger training exercise or drill, the role-players should be given an opportunity to discuss their observations at length because the perspective of the role-players will often mirror the perspective of employees, visitors, and so on who may be involved in an actual emergency situation. For example, envision a drill that concerns evacuating employees from a certain area due to the presence of a suspicious package, and role-players are used to represent the employees. These role-players will have the opportunity to view the security force through the eyes of the employees. Were the security officers calm and professional or disorganized and panicked? These observations will give the instructor insight regarding areas where improvement is needed. It will also help to reaffirm areas where the security force demonstrates competence.

Role-playing can be a valuable part in the training of a security organization. It allows the human dimension to be introduced into training in a way that other methods cannot. It also gives the individual trainee a more realistic feel for the situation. With this background, the trainee will be more familiar with the situation and its associated problems and will be able to respond more effectively. It is up to the individual trainer to determine how to best integrate role-playing into an organization's training program.

# 8

# Exercises to Improve Observation Skills

Among all the qualities security personnel must possess, good observation skills are at the top of the list. Most mission statements for security organizations define their principal duties as deterrence, detection, and reporting. A fundamental element of both detection and reporting is the ability to observe effectively. Observation skills also play a crucial role in the deterrence mission; when a security officer sees an unusual or suspicious person loitering in the building lobby, recognizes the person as a potential threat, and challenges the person as to their business in the building, the deterrence mission is being performed.

Developing observation skills is not as simple as it sounds. Security personnel must be able to keep these skills sharp while maintaining a routine that is often monotonous and dull. Following one training exercise detailed later in this chapter, security officers were asked to write a report reflecting events that they had just witnessed. The response of many was, "I wasn't expecting that," "I don't know, I wasn't paying attention when it happened." The instructor's reply: "Exactly! Incidents occur when they are least expected."

The situation just described is an example of the need for *reactive* observation skills. Reactive observation skills are utilized when a trainee witnesses an incident and can accurately recall the details. Information acquired and reported following an incident can be instrumental to resolving the problem. This is particularly true if the incident was a crime and the police or other law enforcement authorities become involved. Details about a suspect, the clothes they were wearing, and other details can be vitally important. In a situation such as an explosion at the facility, details such as the color of the smoke and the sound of the explosion can help investigators determine what type of explosives were used. There are several good exercises available to train and assess these kinds of reactive observation skills.

The second kind of observation is *proactive*. Observation skills are used proactively when the trainee identifies something out of the ordinary and recognizes it as a possible threat. Examples include the car with no license plates that has been left in front of the building; the gentleman walking into the building with other employees at lunch time who holds up a card that does not appear to be a valid employee ID card; the canvas bag lying against the side of the building; the propped emergency exit door; the envelope bearing multiple stamps and sealed with packing tape addressed to the CEO. The ability to detect these possible problems and realize the need to investigate further are the traits of a professional. Developing this ability in line security personnel will pay great dividends to the organization in terms of preventing many incidents from ever happening. These skills are not only important for security officers. For those personnel providing executive protection, the ability to identify and prevent a problem from occurring, or minimizing it if it does occur, is a key attribute.

The techniques for developing observation skills in security personnel are numerous and limited only by the instructor's imagination. There are, however, some proven methods that should be discussed. Some of these techniques are very old and others relatively new. The key, as with all the exercises in this book, is to take what is useful and applicable, tailor it, and utilize it to develop the security force.

In 1901, British author and poet Rudyard Kipling wrote about "Kim's Game," a technique used to train British intelligence agents in India. Kipling termed it the "jewel game" and described how trainees would be shown piles of stones, swords, daggers, and photographs to memorize and were later tested on the contents (Weale, 1997). This same technique was in use at the Marine Corps Scout Sniper Schools at least as recently as 1992. A version of Kim's Game can be done by showing trainees a set of disparate objects arranged in one room, then bringing the trainees to a separate location and assigning them an unrelated task. When the task is complete, pass out paper and pens and ask the trainees to write down as many as possible of the objects they observed earlier. A different variation of this could use a picture or photograph. Copies of the picture are distributed to the trainees and they are given a specific amount of time to study them, but they may not take notes. The pictures are then collected and the trainees are given a "distractor" task to complete. In some cases, the distractor task may also be a physically demanding task, but this depends upon the organization and mission. The trainees are again asked to list what they saw in the picture.

A different sort of exercise, which helps integrate the confusion and shock of a real incident, requires the use of a videocassette recorder. The instructor can present this as a way to insert practical training into a classroom environment. In this exercise the instructor will use a videotape of an incident. The incident can be drawn from news footage, role-played scenarios on a training tape, archived CCTV surveillance tapes depicting a real incident, or even a scene from a movie. It is helpful if the segment has an audio portion as well, but if there is a narrator giving a voice over, the instructor may wish to turn off the volume. Ideally, the instructor will be delivering a lecture on report writing, observation skills, or some similar topic. The instructor should ensure that all the trainees are positioned where they can see the screen at the beginning of the lecture. At the appropriate time, the instructor should step without warning to the VCR and play the tape. The tape should depict some event that is rapid and confusing. When the event ends, the instructor should turn off the VCR and tell the trainees to write a narrative report describing what they witnessed. When the trainees have finished their reports, the instructor can either spot check several of them, have them exchange them so they may see what others have written, or take volunteers to describe the event. The instructor should then take up position at a chalkboard or overhead projector and ask the trainees questions about the incident. As the trainees answer, the instructor should jot down the answers on the chalkboard or overhead transparency. The instructor may then show the tape a second time to determine the validity of the group's answers. Depending on the amount of time available, the instructor may wish to show the incident several times. Each time the trainees will gain a greater appreciation for both the things they noticed and the things they missed. As mentioned at the beginning of the chapter, the main response of the trainees will probably be that they were not expecting the scenario and were not prepared to view it. Sitting in a lecture class, many of their minds were no doubt wandering and many of them were bored. The reality is that much of the time security work is boring, particularly for the front line employee such as the security officer. The trainee needs to understand that situations in real life will not necessarily announce themselves. They will come unexpectedly, out of the blue, and they will be confusing. By conditioning security personnel to be used to that aspect of security work, the trainer will produce a person more capable of responding effectively.

Another variation on the video exercise involves using one or two assistant instructors as role-players. The assistant instructors enter the classroom and role-play a scenario, and then the trainees are asked to give descriptions of the incident and the participants. An example of this exercise is for the two assistant instructors to burst into the room and simulate assaulting or assassinating the instructor. The instructor can then quiz the class regarding the descriptions and actions of the "assailants." While this variation of the exercise has some advantages—it is more realistic because it involves role-players, not a video—there are also some significant drawbacks. First, unless the assistant instructors are unknown to the trainees or are wearing very elaborate disguises, the trainees' descriptions will be influenced by what they already know about the assistant instructors. Second, there is no way to effectively "replay" the scenario and consequently, the trainees will not receive the same type of feedback and clarification that they will receive from replaying a videotaped incident. Third, if the scenario is too realistic some trainees may not recognize that it is part of the training and may respond as if the situation were real. This is potentially very dangerous. Fourth, this type of training requires considerably more planning and one or two additional instructors than the videotape scenario. Instructors wishing to utilize this technique should plan it thoroughly. Properly conducted, this type of scenario is not only good as a method of improving observation skills, but is also an excellent "attention getter" that can stimulate and rejuvenate the class.

The security trainer may choose to utilize both of these techniques, because each has its strengths and weaknesses. The reality of the role-play based technique is very good, while the video incident allows a greater opportunity for review and dissection. Both of these methods not only improve the trainees' observation skills over time, but they also enhance awareness. The trainee becomes more adept at gathering information quickly and effectively and also gains a better appreciation of the speed with which an incident can occur.

Observation skills can be developed over time. The first step is to make the trainee aware of the need for these skills. The two preceding scenario-based training exercises can help accomplish that mission. At this level, the scenario-based training is primarily geared toward making the trainees more aware of their shortcomings. The next step is to create a building block model where training exercises begin with simple tasks and gradually grow more complex and sophisticated. As with most of the training methods detailed in this book, progression is a key element. The trainee must master simple tasks before moving on to more complex exercises. Using Kim's Game and picture recall exercises will help build a foundation. Later, the scenario-based training can be reintroduced, with an emphasis on improving the trainee's developing observation skills. As the students become more proficient, observation skills training can be integrated with other training exercises as well. For example, a training class on report writing can present the students with a scenario in a similar fashion to the methods mentioned above. The students then have to utilize their observation skills to gather information and write a full incident report, not just a brief narrative. This is very similar to the earlier exercises, except that the report writing skills are the focus here. However, the observation skills are being reinforced as part of the training. This type of complimentary training would be utilized only after the fundamental observation skills were developed.

As the trainees work through observation skills exercises, there should be a noticeable improvement in the quality and completeness of their reports and other work products. This, in addition to performance on the assessment drills already mentioned, should validate the training.

## REFERENCE

Weale, Adrian. *Secret Warfare.* London: Coronet Books, 1997, p. ix.

# 9

# *Testing Training's Effectiveness*

Assuming that the security trainer has conducted the training following a natural progression from simple to more complex, there should be a noticeable improvement in the way security personnel respond on various training exercises. Training must be continually tested and evaluated. The ultimate test of whether or not the training program has accomplished its goal occurs when security personnel respond to a real-world situation. In the absence of a real-world situation, trainers must attempt to make the training more realistic and must increasingly introduce unexpected elements to test the trainees' reactions.

Testing should focus on both emergency response duties and daily functions of the security force. Daily functions would consist of activities such as access control and patrol. More realism can be introduced into the testing of daily functions because this will generally be less disruptive to operations and less likely to result in injuries or other problems. The following outlines are a suggestion for progressive training for emergency response and daily security duties. Some of the same techniques can be used for both types of situations and some are more appropriate for only one type of situation.

**Daily Security Duties**

I. General Lecture on Security Duties
   A. Access Control
   B. Perimeter Patrol
   C. Interior Patrol
   D. Reception Desk
   E. Freight Access Control Point
   F. Security Console/Command Center
   G. Written Exam—Brief 25-question, multiple-choice test on above subjects

II. Post Specific Training (Orientation to each post by trainer and then paired training with security officer assigned to post)
   A. Lobby Access Control Posts—2 hours
   B. Perimeter Patrol—2 hours
   C. Interior Patrol—4 hours
   D. Reception Desk—3 hours
   E. Freight Access Control Point—2 hours
   F. Security Console/Command Center—8 hours

III. Individual Skills Practical Training Test
   A. Demonstrate Access Control Techniques
   B. Demonstrate Perimeter Patrol Techniques
   C. Demonstrate Interior Patrol Techniques
   D. Demonstrate Radio Use
   E. Demonstrate Report Writing/Write Sample Report

IV. Specialist Skills Practical Training Test
   A. Demonstrate Reception Desk Procedures/Pass Issuance
   B. Demonstrate Freight Access/Egress Control Techniques
   C. Demonstrate Security Console Techniques
      1. Monitoring/use of CCTV
      2. Use of facility radio net
      3. Log book entries
      4. Locate emergency contact numbers
      5. Incident report evaluation/filing
      6. Intrusion detection system operation
      7. Remote entrance control operation
      8. Satellite facility communication

 9. Fire/Life Safety System monitoring and response
 V. Role-Play Evaluation (Evaluator assesses each trainee's ability
    to interact with the following types of visitors to the building
    reception desk)
     A. Angry visitor
     B. Hearing-impaired visitor
     C. Foreign language–speaking visitor
VI. Access Control Penetration Exercise (discussed later in this
    chapter)


**Emergency Response Duties**
 I. General Lecture on Emergency Response Procedures
     A. Medical Emergency
     B. Fire
     C. Bomb Threat
     D. Suspicious Item/Suspicious Package
     E. Power Failure
     F. Elevator Entrapment
     G. Riot/Civil Disturbance
     H. Intruder
     I. Written exam—Brief 25-question, multiple-choice test on
        above suspects.
II. Drill Performance Evaluation (In each of these drills, evalua-
    tors accompany the trainees and using a checklist evaluate their
    ability and actions.)
     A. Medical Emergency Drill
     B. Bomb Threat Drill
     C. Suspect Item Drill
     D. Power Failure Drill
     E. Elevator Entrapment Drill
     F. Riot/Civil Disturbance Drill
     G. Intruder Response Drill


These assessment methods have been described more extensively in chapters 2 and 3 dealing with establishing the training

program and chapter 6 conducting realistic drills. The role-play scenarios are particularly useful when testing the daily routine functions that call for effective communication and public relation skills. The next section will deal with penetration testing of the access control program.

## PENETRATION TESTING

In 1984, the U.S. Navy began a bold experiment to test the security of its facilities around the world. A unit known as OP-06D or Naval Security Coordination Team, composed of Navy special warfare personnel, conducted simulated terrorist attacks on Navy bases all over the globe. While many of the exercises involved simulated bombings and hostage takings, it is probably their adeptness at breaching perimeter security and access-control programs that is most applicable to the private sector security practitioner. (Marcinko, Weisman, pp. 281–309).

To penetrate security at Navy installations, the unit used a number of relatively low-tech methods such as climbing fences, both day and night, using false IDs, or simply running through the gate while the guard was distracted. In one notable exercise, the unit was able to enter a base on a high state of alert by riding through the gate hidden in the trunks of taxi cabs (Livingstone, pp. 332–333). The unit did several interesting things during these security evaluations. The "terrorists" were accompanied by a film crew from Essex Corporation to videotape the entire exercise. This assisted in documenting how the facility was breached and recorded some startling lapses in base security. Initially, the group was also accompanied by a lawyer, whose mission was to ensure that nothing that would create a serious liability occurred. This was particularly important during some of the hostage taking sequences, which were frequently very intense (*Red Cell*, 1994).

Not surprisingly, while the unit was very effective at disclosing weaknesses in Navy security, there were many egos bruised in the process. Many base commanders did not appreciate being shown up and rather than viewing the exercises as a constructive process to improve security, they viewed them as damaging to their careers. In March 1986, the unit kidnapped Ron Sheridan, the director of security at Naval Weapons Station, Seal Beach, California. Sheridan was held for approximately 30 hours and underwent a rough physical interrogation. As a result, Sheridan sued both the members of the unit and the Essex Corporation in Los Angeles Federal Court (Livingstone, pp. 335–336). Ironically, the lawyer was not present during this exercise, having been cut for budgetary reasons. By the time the unit was disbanded in 1992, it had seen its activities severely curtailed to conducting tabletop wargaming exercises (*Red Cell*, 1994).

While conducting complex hostage taking exercises is probably not practical or appropriate for the typical security trainer and would probably create an incredible liability exposure, serious consideration should be given to conducting breaching and penetration exercises. These exercises are the best way to practically assess the effectiveness of the access-control program. As with the other training methods described in this book, the penetration testing should be done progressively. The most elementary types of security breaches should be attempted first, and more complex exercises introduced later.

The following steps should be taken to prepare for the penetration exercise:

1. Determine what type of site is to be penetrated. This will dictate the techniques to be used. This information will be enhanced during the reconnaissance phase of the test. At this stage it should be determined if the site is a manufacturing plant, commercial office building, shipping and distribution facility, or other type of site.

2. Determine the type of threat. Is the simulated threat a petty thief, an environmental terrorist group, a former employee? While this may not radically change the exercise, it may dictate some of the techniques used.

3. Designate the members of the penetration team. How many people will be used? The penetration test may be conducted by only one person or may involve several people attempting to enter at various points or various times. Who will they be? Generally speaking, the penetration team cannot be known to the members of the security force or the effectiveness of the exercise will be greatly reduced if not totally destroyed. For proprietary organizations this may pose a difficult problem. Options include considering using personnel from other places, if the organization has multiple facilities. If a contract security service is used, the security services contractor may be able to provide personnel for this purpose. There are also consultants who conduct these exercises for a fee. Whoever is chosen to conduct the penetration test must be trusted individuals. The evaluators are essentially learning how to effectively break into the facility and this could be very damaging knowledge in the wrong hands.

4. Direct the penetration team to reconnoiter the facility (this is optional). In some cases, particularly when conducting more advanced exercises, it may be useful to have the people conducting the exercise gather their own intelligence on the facility. This will allow the security trainer and security manager to also evaluate the awareness of members of the security force. The penetration team should be directed to engage members of the security force in conversation to gather information. If the security personnel divulge too much information and/or fail to report these contacts, the security manager will know there is an awareness problem among members of the security force. This phase is more applicable to advanced penetration tests. In basic tests, the security trainer may wish to brief the penetration team on the layout of the facility and the security procedures.

5. Develop the plan. During this phase, the security trainer and manager, in conjunction with the penetration team, will determine how the security plan should be breached: which entrance

or entrances will be used, what method for gaining entrance will be used, and so on.

6. Decide whether the exercise will be announced or unannounced. While unannounced drills will usually give the most realistic appraisal, only the most fundamental drills can be unannounced. Any drill involving breaching an alarm system or physical barrier such as a fence should be announced. If the security force, or any members of the security force, are armed, the drill should be announced. When announcing the drill, the specific time and place of the drill remain secret. Security force members are informed that the drill is to take place and are given a window of time when it will occur. This is primarily for safety reasons.

7. Set parameters for the exercise and develop safety measures. While realism is important, safety must come first. Parameters must be set to ensure that participants do not become so enthusiastic that they become unsafe.

8. Use a checklist format. Develop a checklist indicating the points to be breached and allowing space for comments by penetration team members.

9. Set a goal for the penetration team. The goal can be as simple as to reach a certain point in the facility and withdraw, or may be as complex as retrieving a certain item and removing it from the facility without being stopped.

10. Provide penetration team members with a letter or pass. It is important to give each of the participants a letter explaining the drill and the participant's role in the drill, particularly if the exercise is unannounced. The letter should give the day or dates that it is effective and it should be signed by the security director, security manager, or some other competent authority and be on organization letterhead. A 24-hour contact phone number should also be included in the letter. In the event that the penetration evaluator is stopped and detained by the security force, the letter may be presented before the security personnel call the police and the situation escalates.

11. Make liaison with local law enforcement authorities if necessary. If any aspect of the drill may come to the attention of local law enforcement authorities, advise them prior to the exercise. For example, if the exercise involves breaching a fence line that runs along a public street, notify the police to prevent the evaluators from being mistaken for burglars and arrested.
12. Notify any central station alarm service providers, if necessary. If the drill involves breaching an alarm system that is connected to an outside central station, notify the service provider in advance of the exercise and have a contact person present to deliver a code word to the central station when the alarm is tripped.
13. For more complex drills, a security department representative such as the security trainer should be in the vicinity. It may be impractical or unrealistic to have the trainer actually visibly present at the facility and may compromise the element of surprise. However, the trainer may take a position in the area and stay in contact with the penetration team during the exercise. The trainer will then be better able to intervene in the event of a problem and may more effectively evaluate the exercise. During more fundamental breaching exercises, the trainer generally need not be present.
14. Conduct a thorough critique. At the conclusion of the exercise, the trainer will want to meet with members of the security force and critique them on their performance. The critique, as always, should take a constructive format. There may be some rare examples where disciplinary action may be taken following an exercise, for example, if security personnel are discovered sleeping on post or involved in gross dereliction of duty. These, however, should be exceptions. There should be every attempt to avoid finger pointing and placing blame during the critique. The focus should be on identifying vulnerabilities within the access-control program and determining how to correct them.
15. Use information gathered during the exercise and critique to plan the next penetration test. Following the concept of pro-

gression, the exercise should be analyzed and a new, more advanced and complex exercise planned. The new exercise should test that measures taken to correct deficiencies discovered in the past test are in place and functional. The new exercise should then attempt to discover new and often less obvious vulnerabilities.

The actual control penetration will be conducted by either of two methods, or in many cases, some combination of the two.

1. *Deception:* Gaining access to the facility through the use of ruses, disguises, or distraction. These exercises are easier to conduct and to integrate into everyday operations. They are, by and large, less disruptive than the second method.
2. *Physical penetration:* Gaining access to the facility by physically evading, defeating, or overcoming physical security measures such as barriers and alarm systems. These exercises are generally more advanced, require greater planning and coordination, and should be conducted after deception exercises have already been used, and corrective measures taken.

The following section outlines examples of three penetration tests of varying degrees of difficulty and complexity. The fictional XYZ Corporation is again used as the setting for these tests.

### Basic Access Control Test

#### Objective
To test the effectiveness of the access-control program in the main lobby of XYZ Corporation headquarters.

#### Situation
Access control in the XYZ main lobby is conducted by means of visual verification of an employee ID card. There is one uniformed security officer posted at each of four elevator banks. The security officer is expected to ensure that all employees entering the elevator

banks display an ID card and that the ID picture matches the person displaying the card.

## Mission
The evaluators will attempt to enter through the main lobby by using ruses and distraction techniques.

## Execution
There will be a team of four evaluators. Each will try to enter during different times and using different methods. These are detailed as follows.

**Evaluator #1** Wearing a business suit and carrying a leather attache case, this evaluator will attempt to walk quickly and determinedly past the security officer during peak morning rush without being challenged. This evaluator will rely on attire, demeanor, and urgency to intimidate or dissuade the security officer into not challenging.

**Evaluator #2** Wearing a shirt and tie and carrying a paper bag of fast food, this evaluator will attempt to pass the security officer during peak lunch hour traffic.

**Evaluators #3 and #4** These evaluators will be dressed in casual attire. Evaluator #3 will approach the security officer and ask for directions. Evaluator #4 will walk quickly past the security officer while the security officer is distracted.

## Goal
The evaluators' goal is to reach the elevator lobby on the fourteenth floor and record the time on their checklist. A security camera on the fourteenth floor will record the evaluators' success.

## Administrative
The evaluators will be equipped with a letter from the security department in the event they are detained. The exercise will be unan-

nounced. A critique will be conducted following the exercise at a time to be designated.

## Advanced Physical Security Breaching Test

### Objective
To test the effectiveness of the physical security program at XYZ Corporation headquarters.

### Situation
The front pedestrian entrance of XYZ Corporation is on Main Street. The vehicle gate for commercial vehicles is located on North Street. The entrance for the employee parking lot is on South Street. The parking lot is split into two parts. The north side is restricted for commercial vehicles, including the company's truck fleet. The south side of the lot is used for employee vehicles. The entire perimeter of the company property is surrounded by a seven-foot chain link fence topped with a triple strand of barbed wire. There is no perimeter alarm system. Located in the rear of the headquarters building is a freight loading dock. The dock is located behind three large rolling gates. The gates are open from 5:00 A.M. to 7:00 P.M. During that time a security officer is posted inside the loading dock area. During off hours the gates are closed. There is a small pedestrian door to one side of the gates. The door is locked after hours. The door has no internal lock and is secured by a chain and padlock. The loading dock area is connected through a short hallway to the main lobby and elevator banks and stairwells. There is a security officer patrolling the perimeter in a golf cart 24 hours a day.

### Mission
The evaluators will attempt to enter the interior of the headquarters building by breaching the physical security program.

### Execution
There will be one evaluator. The evaluator will scale the fence and move to the pedestrian door alongside the gates. The evaluator will

forcibly open the door and proceed to the fire stairwell and use the stairs to proceed to the designated area.

## Goal

The evaluator will retrieve a manila envelope from the reception area on the third floor. The third floor is a reentry floor that can be accessed from the stairwell. The evaluator must then leave the premises undetected.

## Administrative

The evaluator will be equipped with bolt cutters to cut the chain on the pedestrian door. The exercise will be announced and the security force will have a 12-hour window of when the penetration may occur. Local law enforcement authorities will be contacted.

## Access-control Test/Breaching Exercise Incorporating Intelligence Gathering

### Objective

To test the effectiveness of both the access-control program and guard force operational security at XYZ Corporation.

### Situation

The penetration team will assess and consider the entire access-control program at XYZ Corporation.

### Mission

The evaluators/penetration team will gather their own intelligence regarding security at XYZ Corporation and will determine the best way to gain access to the facility. They will then attempt to gain access.

### Execution

The evaluators will attempt to learn as much as possible about operational patterns at XYZ Corporation. This information will be gained by observing the facility over a period of days, engaging building employees and members of the security force in casual conversation and thereby attempting to learn about vulnerabilities that may be exploited. The evaluators will then develop a plan to gain access to the facility using these vulnerabilities. The plan must be reviewed and approved by the instructor to ensure that it is safe

## Goal

The evaluators must attempt to reach the elevator lobby on the twenty-fifth floor. They must also prepare a detailed assessment of the security program based on the intelligence they gathered.

## Administrative

The evaluators will be equipped with a letter explaining their involvement in the exercise. Depending on the method of entry the evaluators choose, the instructor will determine whether the exercise is to be announced or unannounced. The evaluators may use a camera during the intelligence gathering phase. The evaluators must have no prior knowledge about security at the building.

These examples show us three methods that can be used to evaluate the effectiveness of a security program at a given location. In virtually every case, the instructor should start with the most basic type of test and gradually work up to more advanced testing. At some facilities, a breach of a physical security system that involves defeating alarm systems and barriers may not be appropriate or desirable.

Nearly every organization can benefit from a test that involves an intelligence gathering phase. In these exercises, the evaluators must be intelligent, trained people. Their ability to gather information about the security procedures at the facility and to exploit chinks in the armor will give the security department an excellent idea of where to focus their efforts. If the evaluators are able to loiter around the facility, observe patterns of activity and take pictures without being questioned or challenged by members of the security force, a serious vulnerability has been identified.

Likewise, if the evaluators can use social engineering techniques like engaging security and nonsecurity personnel in conversation or using pretext phone calls to gain information about the security of the facility, a problem has been identified. To rectify these problems, the security director should consider improving or expanding the security awareness program, or instituting such a program if it does not already exist.

Documentation of the exercise is very important. Figures 9–1 through 9–3 illustrate the type of documentation that should be used during an access control evaluation/penetration test. These examples are typical of those used for a very basic access-control test. A more advanced or complicated test would require more extensive instructions and documentation. A brief sheet giving the evaluators some basic guidelines to follow when conducting the exercise should be distributed to the penetration team (see Figure 9–1).

An evaluation checklist should be included with the brief sheet. The checklist will ask specific questions for the evaluator to answer regarding time, location, and results of the entry attempt. There should also be a space provided for the evaluator to describe the entry or attempted entry and make additional comments (see Figure 9–2).

As previously mentioned, steps must be taken to ensure that the exercise does not get out of control. Each evaluator should be given a letter describing their participation in the exercise and should include the dates of the exercise. A 24-hour contact number should be included in the letter in case of emergency or any other unforeseen problem (see Figure 9–3).

## DAILY SITUATION TESTING

There may also be a need to evaluate in an objective and unannounced way the security personnel's ability to deal with daily situations. There was discussion in previous chapters 5 and 7 regarding methods of training and developing public relations skills for security officers. Methods included role-playing situations and evaluat-

ACCESS CONTROL EVALUATION/PENETRATION TEST

The goal of this penetration test is to evaluate the effectiveness of the access control
program at XYZ Corporation. This test will identify vulnerabilities that may be
exploited by unauthorized persons attempting to gain access to the building.

XYZ Corporation is located in a twenty-five story building located at 333 Main Street.
The principal entrance for the visitor and employee is located on Main Street. A parking
lot for both employee and commercial vehicles is located in the rear of the building. The
West gate is used by employee vehicles. The East gate is used by commercial vehicles.

Access control in the XYZ lobby is conducted by means of visual verification of an
employee ID card. There is one uniformed security officer posted each of the four
elevator banks. The security officer is expected to ensure that all employees entering the
elevator banks display an ID card and that the ID picture matches the person displaying
the card.

The evaluators will attempt to enter through the main lobby by using ruses and
distraction techniques.

There will be a team of four (4) evaluators:

1. Evaluator #1: Business suit/carrying leather attaché case. Will walk quickly past
   security to elevator banks.

2. Evaluator #2: Shirt and tie/carrying paper bag of fast food. Will attempt to pass
   during lunch hour rush.

3. Evaluators #3 and #4: Casual attire. Will distract security to gain entrance.

Goal: The evaluators' goal is to reach the elevator lobby on the fourteenth floor and
record the time on their checklist.

**Figure 9–1.**   Sample evaluator brief sheet

ing them. These skills can be assessed by using a methodology very
similar to penetration testing. In the retail field this is often known
as "mystery shopping." Evaluators can be sent to the facility posing
as visitors to investigate the demeanor and public relations skills of
security receptionists, lobby security personnel, and others. A similar
checklist can be developed for this purpose. Situations involving
foreign language–speaking visitors can be conducted to determine
how well this situation is handled by security. It is strongly recom-

Evaluation Checklist

Targeted Point of entry: Main Lobby

Date that entry was attempted:_____ Time that entry was attempted:_____

- □ Lobby security personnel were on post.
- □ Lobby security personnel requested evaluator produce I.D.
- □ Lobby security personnel ensured I.D. photograph matched evaluator.
- □ Lobby security personnel refused access to evaluator.
- □ Lobby security personnel allowed evaluator access.
- □ Lobby security personnel denied access but offered to help evaluator (place phone call, etc.) to grant access.

Evaluator rates lobby security personnel as follows:
(5 is best, 1 is worst)

| | | | | |
|---|---|---|---|---|
| Vigilance: | 1 | 2 | 3 | 4 | 5 |
| Appearance: | 1 | 2 | 3 | 4 | 5 |
| Assertiveness: | 1 | 2 | 3 | 4 | 5 |
| Public Relations: | 1 | 2 | 3 | 4 | 5 |

Description/Comments:

_____
_____
_____
_____
_____
_____
_____

Evaluator:_____

Signature:_____

Date:_____

**Figure 9–2.** Sample evaluation checklist

mended that difficult customer-type situations not be simulated. These may place undue stress on staff members and may impede real-world operations. Mystery shopping-type evaluations should be designed to be as unobtrusive as possible.

## XYZ CORPORATION

ANYTOWN, USA 12345

XYZ Security Personnel:

Please be advised that _____ is taking part in an evaluation of the security program at XYZ Corporation. In this capacity, he/she may attempt to breach security. This test has been designated for the date(s)_____. Please contact myself or Peter Harris via pager twenty-four hours a day at 000-111-0101 if you have any questions.

Thank you for your assistance.

Sincerely,

Joseph Williams
Director of Security

**Figure 9–3.**  Sample evaluator letter

When considering implementing any of these practical evaluation methods the trainer should consider the culture of the organization and seek guidance from upper management. What may be appropriate and effective at one company or type of facility may create a serious problem at another. Safety and liability concerns should also be given close attention. While realistic training is important, safety should never be compromised. Finally, the threats that are to be simulated should conform with a realistic threat assessment of the organization. By applying these tools progressively, the trainer can take a proactive step towards dramatically improving security and awareness.

## CRITIQUING

Following an access-control evaluation exercise, the instructor will want to conduct a critique. This can happen the next day or several days later. The instructor will want to review the evaluation checklists, debrief the evaluators and, if possible, view any close circuit camera tapes that may depict the penetration or attempted penetration. In the vast majority of cases, the facility will use a closed circuit camera system covering points of access and egress. Frequently, these cameras will videotape the breaching exercise step by step. The tape may then be replayed and compared to the checklists and the evaluators' comments. Having digested this information, the instructor will be ready to meet with the security staff members involved in the exercise and perhaps other management representatives from the security department.

As always, the critique should be conducted in a positive, constructive fashion. If the breach was unsuccessful, the security staff should be acknowledged for their vigilance. If the evaluators were able to gain access, areas for improvement should be addressed. On some occasions, the evaluation may uncover a serious dereliction of duty. This may involve members of the security force sleeping on post, ignoring their duties or, in some cases, not being on post at all. In these situations, the security department must take some type of corrective measure to address the problem. This will usually take the form of counseling, disciplinary action, and sometimes even termination. These matters should be resolved apart from, and preferably prior to, the critique. The critique should not become a forum for meting out disciplinary action. It is important that the critique be conducted in the proper spirit. It is very easy for line employees to view an access control evaluation of this type as management's attempt to "spy" on them. The need for effective evaluation of the security program must be explained to the security staff. Evaluation exercises of this sort are not only directed toward finding employee error by the security personnel, but may also detect poor policies and security systems problems. The exercise should be viewed as a positive experience that, like the drills discussed earlier, will allow training and policies to be realistically tested so that problems may be found sooner, rather than later. This type of proactive approach benefits everyone from the CEO to the line employee.

## REFERENCES

Livingstone, Neil C. *The Cult of Counterterrorism*. Lexington: Lexington Books, 1990, pp. 332–333, 335–336.

Marcinko R., and Weisman, J. *Rogue Warrior.* New York: Pocket Books, 1992, pp. 281–309.

———. *Red Cell: The True Story*. L.O.T.I. Films, 1994.

———. *FM 34–60 Counterintelligence.* Headquarters Department of the Army, Washington, D.C., October 3, 1995.

# 10

# *Training Management and Specialized Personnel*

The same principles of practical training can be applied to the training of security staff members such as investigators, executive protection personnel and security drivers, EMTs, and management personnel. The techniques must be used appropriately for each category of employee.

## INVESTIGATORS

Investigators in the security department of a large company often have little free time. When down time is available, the manager will want to utilize training techniques that provide the maximum result in the minimum time. Different types of techniques may be utilized when training new, as opposed to veteran, investigators. The trainee may be presented with either a case study or a hypothetical situation that depicts the type of internal investigations that occur at the organization. When presented with this scenario, the investigator must come up with an investigative plan. The plan will detail the steps to be taken in the investigation, what information is needed, and who will be interviewed. The instructor can then introduce other information into the scenario and direct the investigator to write a report. In some cases, the trainer may wish to role-play interview of interrogation sessions with the investigator.

For the more experienced investigator, the situations and case studies should be more complex. Since liability issues are a very important consideration when conducting investigations, situations can be drawn from case law. By understanding potential legal pitfalls that may be present in an investigation, the investigator will be better prepared to navigate around these hazards. The following is an example of a case study that may be useful in investigative training.

### Case Study: Legal Issues for Investigators

During a bank employee's absence from work, coworkers discovered $3,220 missing from a vault. The bank investigator, in conjunction with a state police investigator, interviewed the woman as part of the investigation. By the time the interview ended, the woman had confessed. She pleaded not guilty to grand larceny and the charges were later dismissed. She subsequently filed a lawsuit against the bank and police officer "claiming that they acted in concert in coercing the confession in violation of the fifth amendment privilege against self incrimination."

Evidence at the trial indicated that the bank investigator, who was physically larger than the plaintiff, behaved in a loud, aggressive manner and threatened to reveal the investigation to her family and her husband's employer in order to coerce her confession.

The jury found in favor of the plaintiff. Ultimately, the bank settled for $150,000 and the damages against the police officer were reduced from $200,000 to $40,000. (*AELE Security Legal Update*, *Niemann v. Whalen*, 928F.supp 296, S.D.N.Y.)

1. How could the interview have been conducted to reduce liability?
2. What impact did the presence of the police officer have? Was the bank acting as an "agent of the police"?

## EXECUTIVE PROTECTION PERSONNEL

Executive protection (EP) personnel can benefit a great deal from using case studies and case study-based drills. Classroom study of incidents of assassination, kidnapping, and assault can assist EP personnel in better identifying the types of threats that exist. This also will provide them with an opportunity to place themselves in the situation and consider how they would respond. These case studies can be taken a step further by using them as a foundation for drills. When the EP team has down time they may conduct drills to demonstrate a response to various situations.

For some of the exercises a role-player may be used to simulate the principal. Advance work exercises can also be conducted to train personnel to prepare a location for the principal's arrival—security drivers and security-trained executive chauffeurs are a subcategory of executive protection personnel and can be trained using many of the same techniques. Case studies of vehicle attacks are particularly valuable in this regard. The Alfred Herrhausen incident mentioned in Chapter 4 is a good example. Considering that statistically most attacks occur while the victim is in transit, there is an abundance of cases to review. This prevalence also makes the effective training of security drivers all the more important.

## MEDICAL PERSONNEL

EMTs and other personnel specially trained to respond to medical emergencies can be trained using a variety of practical techniques. Role-playing can describe a variety of problems or symptoms for them to simulate treating. Likewise, during an emergency drill, the instructor can assess casualties and place a card on each of the "injured" people. Each card will describe the wound and the trainee will have to describe a method for handling the first aid treatment.

### Scenario

A bomb placed in a knapsack explodes outside the entrance to XYZ Corporation Headquarters at 8:45 A.M. Many employees are entering the building at that time. The bomb is a crude device using black-powder in a coffee can with bolts and screws packed into it for shrapnel. Ten employees are injured in the blast. Emergency medical services are notified. While they await the ambulances, several XYZ security officers who are cross-designated as EMTs respond to the injured people.

### Response

The instructor gives each of the ten role-players a "casualty card." The card describes the nature of the injuries that they have. The cards are attached to a long cord and worn around the "victims" necks. The EMTs must assess and provide aid to each of the victims. Some example cards are:

1. Conscious/immobile. Multiple puncture wounds on left arm.
2. Unconscious. Multiple puncture wounds to head, chest, and legs.
3. Conscious/immobile. Multiple puncture wounds and burns on both legs.
4. Unconscious. Lacerations on face and head. Heavy bleeding.
5. Conscious/immobile. Multiple puncture wounds in back and legs. Burns to back and legs. Lacerations from broken glass on hands and arms. Heavy bleeding. Shock.
6. Conscious/mobile. Puncture wounds on arms and hands.
7. Conscious/mobile. Puncture wounds to left arm and leg.
8. Unconscious/cardiac arrest. No external wound.
9. Conscious/immobile. Puncture wounds to back and legs, lacerations from broken glass to back and legs.
10. Conscious/immobile. Puncture wounds to right leg.

## MANAGEMENT PERSONNEL

Management personnel can also be effectively trained and developed by using practical techniques. In these situations, junior leaders can be separated from the rest of the security department for a day, and presented with hypothetical situations and case studies to consider. These scenarios can take two forms:

1. *Practical operations scenarios:* The situation presented simulates a security incident or issue that must be responded to. For example, a suspicious package found in the building lobby, a flood in the sub-basement, or a workplace violence incident. The trainee then must determine the proper steps to take to resolve or control the situation. The walk through, talk through exercise involving the chemical spill discussed in Chapter 5 is a good example of this type of training.
2. *Leadership/ethics scenarios:* These situations have more to do with human relations and dealing with subordinates. This type of training is as critical for management as it is for supervisors. While managers often enjoy the advantage of greater separation from line employees, and are generally less conflicted when dealing with them, many similar concerns are still present.

Security management personnel should be particularly trained to deal with situations that may not be clearly outlined in procedures manuals. By considering possible threats and discussing plans to deal with them, management personnel can "learn to think" and be better prepared when these events do occur.

Management training can be conducted further individually or in groups. Managers should be encouraged to begin a professional education or professional reading program. Situations taken from these readings can form the basis of an ongoing management development program.

## Command Post Exercises

Large security departments may want to consider conducting command post exercises. These exercises simulate response to a crisis situation. While the scenario is usually constructive (that is, it is not being role-played—it can, however, be integrated into a larger drill involving line employees or role-playing), the management and supervisory elements of the security department carry out the decision-making and communications tasks that they would normally perform in such situations. The security department's response would be limited to containing and managing the situation until it can be turned over to public agencies like police and fire department personnel. In some cases, particularly with isolated facilities that are more self-contained, it may be appropriate to simulate managing the process from start to finish. In addition to management personnel, console communication functions should be included in the command post exercise.

Some situations that can be used when conducting a command post exercise are:

1. Natural disaster
   a. Flood
   b. Blizzard
   c. Tornado
   d. Fire
   f. Earthquake
2. Power outage
3. Bomb threat
4. Civil disturbance/riot
5. Labor strike
6. Armed intruder within facility
7. Mass casualty situation
8. Explosion
9. Theft
10. Hazardous materials incident

When conducting a command post exercise, some of the following actions may be simulated:

1. Dispatching personnel to various points
2. Liaison with public agencies
3. Notification within organization—calling key personnel, activating a phone tree

4. Establishing alternate headquarters—implementing business continuity plans
5. Isolating effected portions of the facility
6. Communicating with remote sites and satellite facilities
7. Arranging transportation for people or assets
8. Supervising a search of the facility (for injured personnel, a bomb, etc.)

**Example Exercise**

**Participants**    Security director, security manager, 8-to-4 shift supervisor, 8-to-4 shift console operator, two security officers.

**Scenario**    Due to an unpopular verdict in a highly publicized and controversial criminal trial, rioting and general civil unrest has begun in a neighborhood adjacent to the downtown business district. The police are responding but are unprepared for the size of the crowd and are unable to control it. In view of this situation, the security director designates the security console room as the command post and shifts the security operation into a crisis-response mode.

**Response**    Possible actions to be taken as part of the command post exercise include:

1. Notification of XYZ Corporation management.
2. Notification to security personnel to remain on duty until further notice due to the situation.
3. Notification to company employees that a potentially dangerous situation exists outside and a recommendation that all employees remain within the building.
4. Dispatch security officers to close all entrances except the main entrance and concentrate security personnel at the main entrance.

5. Contact the 4-to-12 shift supervisor and shift personnel at home and notify them to meet at a designated rally point off-site in a safe area. From the rally point, the 4-to-12 shift members will move to the site as a group.
6. Designate the safest possible route for the 4-to-12 shift team from the rally point to the building.
7. Bring the 4-to-12 shift team members in as soon as possible to reinforce the 8-to-4 shift.
8. Keep both shifts on duty until the crisis is resolved.
9. Notify the 12-to-8 shift supervisor and shift members and instruct them to meet at the rally point one hour prior to the start of their shift.
10. Notify the 8-to-4 shift supervisor to have emergency firefighting and medical equipment accessible.
11. Post watches on an upper floor or building roof to observe the actions and movement of the crowd.

Throughout the command post drill the participants will actually contact or simulate contact with the required parties. The participants may wish to use a security officer to represent outside agencies and upper management that must be contacted. The security officer can receive the phone calls from the command post and simulate the interaction with the caller. Attempts should be made to actually telephone the shift supervisor and shift members at home. This will help identify problems such as telephone number changes and disconnected telephone numbers that may not have been previously known. It also will give management a realistic feel for how many personnel can be effectively contacted and summoned to work in the event of an emergency. It should be recognized that some of the security personnel may reside in or near the area where the unrest is occurring and may be unable or unwilling to report to work for safety reasons.

## Crisis Management Team Exercises

Similar to the command post exercise is a crisis management team (CMT) exercise. The two can be performed in conjunction with each other, separately, or as part of a large-scale drill. Many large organizations utilize the crisis management team concept. Crisis management teams generally include members from various parts of the organization, including security Facilities, building maintenance, legal, telecommunications, and representatives may all play a role on the crisis management team. CMT training can be conducted in a similar manner to traditional post exercises. Because the CMT tends to be composed of influential people from various departments within the organization, it is probably not the ideal place to initially experiment with these techniques. However, after practicing and achieving success with other practical training exercises within the security department, the security director may wish to suggest this type of training for the CMT.

Crisis management team training can utilize several practical training techniques. Two of the best are case studies and hypothetical scenarios. Case studies of problems that occurred at similar companies are excellent for training CMT personnel. As mentioned earlier, one of the great advantages of case studies is that they eliminate the need to create a realistic hypothetical scenario because they are, by definition, real-world scenarios. This can reduce criticism that the scenarios are unrealistic and will encourage the participants to take a more serious approach to the training because its relevance is apparent. Of course, the case study must be relevant to the organization conducting the training.

Some areas of concern that may be addressed by crisis management teams are:

1. Natural disaster/business continuity operations
2. Theft of intellectual property
3. Kidnapping of company personnel
4. Sabotage of information systems
5. Hazardous materials incident
6. Threats against company or executives
7. Product counterfeiting
8. Product diversion
9. White collar crime/fraud/embezzlement
10. Bomb incidents

11. Evacuation of company personnel from high risk areas abroad

## Example Exercise

The following is an example of a crisis management team exercise. Once again, the company in question is the XYZ Corporation. The situation is a hypothetical scenario of the type of crisis the CMT for a large company with multinational operations may confront.

**Scenario**   John Jacobs is the manager for XYZ Corporation's new branch office in Bogota, Colombia. The branch office has a small staff of seven people: two other U.S. citizens besides Jacobs and four Colombian nationals. On April 7, XYZ headquarters receives a call from Helen Murphy, XYZ's number two person in Bogota. Murphy states that Jacobs has not arrived at work and there is no answer at his home phone. Later the same day, Murphy calls back to inform XYZ headquarters that the Bogota branch office has received a call from a man claiming to be affiliated with the M-19 leftist guerilla group. The man stated that the M-19 had seized Jacobs and would release him in exchange for a five million dollar ransom. Murphy later received a call from Jacobs's neighbor, a foreign diplomat, who observed Jacobs being forced into a car that morning by three men as he left his home. The neighbor notified the local police at that time. Colombian law forbids payment of ransom or negotiating with kidnappers.

**Response**   Issues for the crisis management team to consider:

1. Public agencies to make liaison with:
   a. U.S. State Department
   b. Federal Bureau of Investigation
   c. Colombian law enforcement authorities
2. Will liaison with any of those agencies limit the options available to XYZ Corporation?
3. Does XYZ Corporation have kidnap and ransom insurance? What are the terms of the policy?

4. Should XYZ Corporation retain a private firm with experience in kidnapping negotiation?
5. What are the implications if XYZ Corporation violates Colombian law and negotiates or pays ransom to the kidnappers?
6. Have there been similar incidents where corporate personnel have been kidnapped and later released safely in Colombia?
7. If so, could persons and/or companies involved in those incidents be contacted for advice and insight on resolving the situation?
8. In these incidents, was M-19 involved or another group?
9. What additional protective measures should be taken to protect the remaining XYZ corporate staff in Bogota?
10. Should these measures be applied to XYZ personnel assigned elsewhere in the region?
11. Will payment of a ransom encourage future kidnappings of XYZ personnel in Colombia and neighboring countries?

The crisis management team must consider each of these concerns as they plan how to successfully resolve the crisis. By reviewing scenarios of this type, the CMT not only becomes more adept at problem solving when situations arise, it may also proactively identify areas to correct. These proactive steps may include increasing security measures for employees assigned abroad, particularly in high-risk areas. If the CMT considers employing the services of a firm specializing in kidnap negotiations, this service can be researched prior to an incident occurring. By locating a qualified firm and making liaison proactively, the company will be more capable of a smooth, effective response should this situation arise.

The same principles apply when dealing with any of the other threats the CMT may face. This allows the CMT to identify the necessary contacts among public agencies, consulting firms, and vendors and consider the insurance ramifications and legal aspects prior to being confronted with the crisis.

Management training should be a continuous process as time permits. Clearly, an organization's leadership is often busy dealing with real problems on a day-to-day basis and may have little time to consider hypothetical problems. The security director may wish to take a few hours per month, or even on a bimonthly or quarterly basis, to sit down with the managers and supervisors within the security department. At these meetings, case studies can be discussed and the participants can consider how their organization would respond under similar circumstances. Serious thought should be given to the preparation for these meetings. The security director, security trainer, or other designated person should be assigned to research a case study relating to a certain type of situation and present it to the others. Visual aids such as handouts and videotapes should be used whenever possible.

These meetings may also help build a foundation for drills and training exercises involving the security force. In this way, the concepts of practical training can be used to build a stronger, more professional security organization from top to bottom.

## REFERENCE

Seger, Karl A. *The Antiterrorism Handbook*. Novato, CA: Presidio Press, 1990.

# 11

# *Individual Applications of Practical Training*

Throughout this book, practical training has been discussed from the perspective of the organization. Practical training principles can be applied by individual security professionals every day to improve their performance and ability to respond to an emergency. The critical aspect of individual training is that the person must be motivated, self-disciplined, and constantly seeking to prepare for the unexpected.

The individual security practitioner can use a technique known as mind-setting to prepare for possible crises. Gary Cunningham and Mike Wallace in their article "Games to Play," point out that most security personnel have significant down time or uneventful periods that can be used constructively. By examining their surroundings and knowing the threats that exist, security personnel can envision possible scenarios and visualize how they would respond. By realistically imagining how an incident could take place and determining the best ways to respond, the security practitioner is becoming better prepared to cope with the situation. Not only is the person intellectually training themselves to respond, they are also psychologically and emotionally preparing to deal with the crisis.

One of the best examples of practical training principles being put to work on the individual level is Sanford Strong's book *Strong on Defense.* Sanford Strong, who may be familiar to some readers from his appearances on television's *America's Most Wanted*, is a former San Diego police officer and law enforcement instructor. His area of expertise is survival skills development. On the *America's Most Wanted* program, Strong typically narrates a role-play scenario of a violent crime occurring. Strong then breaks down the scenario and critiques how the role-players responded. The incident is shown a second time with the role-players depicting a more effective response to the situation.

*Strong on Defense* is directed toward personal and family protection against violent crime. Strong provides case studies of various violent crimes and analyzes how the victim responded. Some case studies include comments made by the victim. While *Strong on Defense* is oriented toward personal protection, not institutional security, the methodology used is pure practical training. Strong places a significant emphasis on mind-setting as a method of psychologically preparing for a shocking or traumatic experience. By mentally rehearsing situations over and over, the person is better able to overcome their fear and surprise and take action to resolve the situation.

This kind of mind-setting applies not only to responding to violent crime but also to any of the emergency situations that have been mentioned throughout this book. If the security officer is standing post and contemplates how to react if a fire alarm were suddenly received, that same security officer will be less startled and less confused if the alarm is activated. If the situation required the security officer to respond to another part of the facility, the security officer could envision the quickest, safest route to use.

At this level, many of the same techniques, such as case studies and hypothetical situations, are simply being applied on an individual, rather than a group level. The instructor can suggest mind-setting techniques to the trainees, but ultimately this is an individual activity and some trainees will prefer daydreaming to preparing themselves to face some unseen threat. Motivated personnel will apply mind-setting techniques outside the work environment to help ensure their own personal safety. These methods will also create a more enhanced security awareness. As the security personnel become more aware of their surroundings, they will be more likely to detect unusual activity that may signal a threat.

## REFERENCES

Cunningham, G., and Wallace, M. "Games to Play." *Informed Source*, September, 1997.

Strong, Sanford. *Strong on Defense*. New York: Pocket Books, 1996.

# 12

# Resources for Security Trainers

Security trainers must be able to draw on a variety of sources to help make their programs interesting and relevant. Information for case studies exercises can often be culled from everyday sources like newspapers and magazines. Many times, however, trainers will need more specific information to meet their needs. Therefore, trainers need to be aware of the resources that exist. These resources include organizations and professional associations, magazines and newsletters, books, training schools, and Internet web sites. Many of these resources are interconnected; for example, a professional association may offer training classes and seminars, host a web site, and publish a magazine or trade journal.

Resources vary in terms of quality, accessibility, and relevance. No single trainer has the time or need to belong to every association, read every periodical and book, and attend every seminar. The goal for the trainer is to seek out the resources that are needed at that particular time and by that particular organization.

The following guide is an attempt to make trainers in the security field aware of some of the resources available. This is not intended to be an endorsement of these resources, nor is it intended to be an all inclusive list. Information changes daily and there are constantly new sources of information appearing in the industry. Every attempt has been made to be as accurate as possible

## ASSOCIATIONS

The associations listed are representative of various disciplines within security, training, or in some cases, both.

### American Society for Industrial Security

This organization of practitioners for all sectors of the security industry is one of the oldest, best respected, and most professional organizations around. In addition to offering numerous seminars and training programs, ASIS consists of numerous chapters throughout the United States and the world where security professionals can meet and exchange information. ASIS publishes *Security Management* magazine on a monthly basis. ASIS also administers the Certified Protection Professional program, whereby qualified applicants are tested in various security disciplines and if successful, are certified by the organization. The ASIS O.P. Norton Information Resource Center contains a library of security books and periodicals that are invaluable to the trainer and can be borrowed free by ASIS members.

Contact information:

American Society for Industrial Security

1625 Prince Street

Alexandria, VA 22314-2818

Telephone: 703-519-6200

Fax: 703-518-1518

Web site: http://www.asisonline.org

### Academy of Security Educators and Trainers

This organization is composed of security trainers and those teaching security classes at colleges and other institutions. The Academy conducts a three-day annual conference for trainers and publishes a newsletter, *The Educator.* The organization also grants the Certified Security Trainer designation to those who complete a five-day assessment and evaluation program consisting of written and oral examinations, workshops, and three training presentations performed before the certification board.

Contact information:

Academy of Security Educators and Trainers

P.O. Box 802

Berryville, VA 22611-0802

Telephone: 540-554-2547

## American Society of Law Enforcement Trainers

This very professional organization may appeal to security trainers in organizations that more closely connect with public law enforcement agencies, for example, college campus security organizations. It publishes *The Law Enforcement Trainer* magazine, in which many articles deal with defensive tactics training and firearms training. This may be helpful for organizations that use armed personnel or personnel who perform high-risk functions. Articles on training techniques and methods may be valuable to all trainers. This association may be less relevant to those in other fields of security.

Contact information:

American Society of Law Enforcement Trainers

102 Dock Road

P.O. Box 361

Lewes, DE 19958-0361

Telephone: 302-645-4080

Fax: 302-645-4084

### American Society for Training and Development

This organization includes trainers in many fields. The society publishes *Training and Development* magazine, *Technical Training*, and *Human Resources Development Quarterly*. Additional services include conferences, seminars, and networking opportunities.

Contact information:

American Society for Training and Development

1640 King Street, Box 1443

Alexandria, VA 22313-2043

Telephone: 703-683-8100

Fax: 703-683-1523

Web site: http://www.astd.org/virtual_community/

### International Foundation for Protection Officers

An association oriented towards uniformed line security personnel, IFPO administers the Certified Protection Officer and Certified Security Supervisor credentials. Both of these programs are by correspondence. They also publish the quarterly newsletter *Protection News*, training manuals, and booklets.

Contact information:

International Foundation for Protection Officers

Suite 200

4200 Meridian

Bellingham, WA 98226

Telephone: 360-733-1571

Fax: 360-671-4329

Web site: http://www.ifpo.com

### *International Association of Professional Security Consultants*

This organization may be of interest to trainers who are independent consultants. The association publishes the newsletter *Independent Consultant*.

Contact Information:

International Association of Professional Security Consultants

1444 I Street, NW

Suite 700

Washington, DC 20005-2210

Telephone: 202-712-9043

Fax: 202-216-9646

Web site: http://www.IAPSC.org

### *International Association for Counterterrorism and Security Professionals*

This is an organization of government, private, and military security practitioners that publishes The *Journal of Counterterrorism & Security International* quarterly and the *Counterterrorism & Security Reports* bimonthly newsletter. The focus is on domestic and international terrorism, international crime, and security techniques.

Contact information:

International Association for Counterterrorism and Security Professionals

P.O. Box 10265

Arlington, VA 22210

Telephone: 703-243-0993

Fax: 703-243-1197

Web site: http://www.securitynet.com

### Association of Certified Fraud Examiners

This organization is composed of investigators, auditors, security managers, accountants, and others concerned about all types of fraud. The association publishes a magazine, *White Paper*, which includes, among other things, many case studies of fraud. ACFE also runs many training seminars and correspondence courses. Many of these classes use the case-study methodology to describe how various frauds were perpetrated. The association administers the Certified Fraud Examiner program, where qualified candidates take a computer-based exam to gain certification.

Contact information:

Association of Certified Fraud Examiners

The Gregor Building

716 West Avenue

Austin, Texas 78701

Telephone: 512-478-9070

Fax: 512-478-9297

Web site: http://www.cfenet.com

### International Association of Law Enforcement Firearms Instructors

Trainers who work with armed security forces or are otherwise involved with firearms instruction may be interested in this organization. IALEFI publishes a magazine called *The Firearms Instructor* and sponsors regional and national seminar programs.

Contact information:

International Association of Law Enforcement Firearms Instructors

25 Country Club Road

Suite 707

Gilford, NH 03246

Phone: 603-524-8787

Fax: 603-524-0076

Web site: www.palen.com

## *International Society of Crime Prevention Practitioners*

An association of crime prevention practitioners in the public and private sectors, ISCPP offers training programs and several publications, including *The Practitioner.*

Contact information:

International Society of Crime Prevention Practitioners

266 Sandy Point Road

Emlenton, PA 16373

Telephone: 724-867-1000

Fax: 724-867-1200

Web site: http://www.ourworld.compuserve.com/homepages/iscpp/

## *International Association for Healthcare Security and Safety*

This organization consisting of security professionals employed by hospitals and other healthcare facilities holds an annual meeting, presents training programs, and publishes *The Journal of Healthcare Protection Management.*

Contact information:

International Association for Healthcare Security and Safety

P.O. Box 637

Lombard, Illinois 60148

Telephone: 630-953-0990

Fax: 630-953-1786

Web site: http://www.iahss.org

## International Association of Campus Law Enforcement Administrators

This organization is composed of college and university security managers and campus police administrators. An annual conference is held and publications include *The Campus Law Enforcement Journal.*

Contact information:

International Association of Campus Law Enforcement Administrators

342 North Main Street

West Hartford, CT 06117-2507

Telephone: 860-586-7517

Fax: 860-586-7550

Web site: http://www.iaclea.org

## Association of Contingency Planners

An organization of emergency managers, contingency planners, and others concerned with disaster mitigation, this association may be helpful for trainers who do a considerable amount of emergency response training. Publishes *The Sentinel.*

Contact information:

ACP Membership Services

7040 S. 13th Street

Oak Creek, WI 53154

Telephone: 414 768 8000, ext. 116

Web site: http://www.acp international.com

## International Computer Security Association

This organization of computer security professionals publishes *Information Security* magazine.

Contact information:

ICSA Professional Membership

1200 Walnut Bottom Road

Carlisle, PA 17013-7635

Telephone: 717-241-3250

Fax: 717-243-8642

Web site: http://www.icsa.net

## American Management Association

The AMA offers courses and publications of value to trainers and instructors.

Contact information:

American Management Association

1601 Broadway

New York, NY 10019-7420

Telephone: 1-800-262-9099

Web site: http://www.amanet.org

## SCHOOLS AND TRAINING PROGRAMS

The schools and training programs mentioned focus on a number of disciplines within the security field, from interview and interrogation to firearms and defensive tactics skills. Some may be of interest simply as a referral or a resource, and others offer instructor certification programs that can enhance the trainer's credentials.

### Crisis Prevention Institute, Inc.

CPI offers one- and two-day workshops on nonviolent crisis intervention. A four-day instructor certification program is also available. CPI-certified instructors are authorized to teach CPI nonviolent crisis intervention techniques at their own organizations. Extensive support services are available to newly certified instructors. With the rising concern with workplace violence, many security instructors may be interested in these programs. CPI training teams present the programs throughout the United States.

Contact information:

Crisis Prevention Institute

3315-K N. 124th Street

Brookfield, WI 53005

Telephone: 1-800-558-8976

Fax: 414-783-5906

Web site: http://www.execpc.com/~cpi

### John E. Reid and Associates, Inc.

This is a respected provider of training courses on interview and interrogation skills. Regular and advanced courses are offered at cities throughout the United States.

Contact information:

John E. Reid and Associates, Inc.

250 Wacker Drive, Suite 1100

Chicago, IL 60606

Telephone: 1-800-755-5747

Fax: 312-876-1713

## Wicklander-Zulawski & Associates, Inc.

This group offers interview and interrogation seminars licensed by John E. Reid and Associates, Inc. Seminars are held in cities around the United States. Seminars in sexual harassment interviewing and employment prescreening are also offered.

Contact information:

Wicklander-Zulawski & Associates, Inc.

4932 Main Street

Downers Grove, IL 60515-3611

Telephone: 1-800-222-7789

Fax: 630-852-7081

## Interviews Interrogation Institute

This is a California-based school for interview and interrogation training.

Contact information:

Interviews Interrogations Institute

P.O. Box 1023

Orangevale, CA 95662

Telephone: 916-722-8282

Web site: http://www.iiiconfess.com

### Scotti School

This respected school focuses on evasive driving skills for executive protection personnel. Courses include protective driving, surveillance detection, security driver seminars, and executive protection. Some courses are held in conjunction with Heckler & Koch. Headquarters are in Massachusetts with training facilities in Michigan, Florida, Peru, and Switzerland.

Contact information:

Scotti School

10 High Street, Suite 15

Medford, MA 02155

Telephone: 1-800-343-0046

Fax: 781-391-8252

Web site: http://www.ssdd.com

### Executive Protection Institute

Training courses for executive protection personnel are offered at this Virginia-based school. Founded by Dr. Richard Kobetz in 1978, EPI teaches basic protection courses and specialized courses in aircraft and maritime security and advance work. A series of two-day seminar programs are also offered throughout the United States. EPI also offers several books and other publications.

Contact information:

Richard W. Kobetz & Associates, Ltd.

Executive Protection Institute

P.O. Box 802

Berryville, VA 22611

Telephone: 540-955-1128

Fax: 540-955-0255

Web site: http://www.personalprotection.com

### Executive Security International, Ltd.

ESI provides executive protection training similar in format to the courses at EPI. ESI also offers courses on investigative techniques, maritime and yacht security, hotel, resort and cruise line casino security, and security operations. ESI offers an accredited associate degree. Interestingly, ESI President Bob Duggan is a former Marxist revolutionary who was active in Latin America prior to changing sides.

Contact information:

Executive Security International

2101 Emma Road

Basalt, CO 81621

Telephone: 1-800-874-0888

Web site: http://www.esi-lifeforce.com

### Smith & Wesson Academy

Renowned firearms training school that offers courses for both law enforcement and private security personnel. Several nonfirearms courses are offered on topics like defense tactics, weapons retention, OC spray, and expandable batons. Numerous instructor certifications in various disciplines are offered.

Contact information:

Smith & Wesson Academy

2100 Roosevelt Avenue

Springfield, MA 01102-2208

Telephone: 413 781-8300

Fax: 413-736-0776

Web site: http://www.smith-wesson.com/academy/

### Heckler & Koch International Training Division

Firearms manufacturer H & K's training academy offers courses similar to the Smith & Wesson Academy.

Contact information:

Heckler & Koch, Inc.

International Training Division

21480 Pacific Boulevard

Sterling, VA 20166-8903

Telephone: 703-450-1900

Fax: 703-406-2361

### Gunsite

This famous Arizona-based firearms training school offers numerous courses for armed personnel.

Contact information:

Gunsite

P.O. Box 700

Paulden, AZ 86334-0700

Telephone: 520-636-4565

Web site: http://www.gunsite.net

### Rape Aggression Defense Systems

The R.A.D. program is taught to students at over 350 colleges and universities and is endorsed by the International Association of Campus Law Enforcement Administrators. Rape Aggression Defense Systems instructor certification courses are also available.

Contact information:

R.A.D. Systems

498-A Wythe Creek Road

Poquoson, VA 23662

Telephone· 1-888-472-3543

Fax· 757-868-4401

Web site: http://www.rad-systems.com

## CDT Training, Inc.

CDT offers Compliance-Direction-Takedown defensive tactics training for law enforcement and private security personnel. This non-deadly force training is designed to protect the practitioner against both the assailant and the lawsuit that may follow. Several instructor certification courses specifically designed for security personnel are offered.

Contact information:

CDT Training, Inc.

281 Route 46 West

Elmwood Park, NJ 07407

Telephone: 201-475-1136

Fax: 201-475-1119

Web site: http://www.cdt-training.com

## GPU Nuclear

Training for security and law enforcement personnel includes OSHA and HAZMAT training, defensive tactics, and FATS firearm simulator training. Facilities are in Pennsylvania and New Jersey.

Contact information:

GPU Nuclear

P.O. Box 480

Middletown, PA 17057

Telephone: 717-948-2045

Fax: 717-948-2058

### R.E.B. Security Training, Inc.

R.E.B. offers training and certification in management of aggressive behavior.

Contact information:

R.E.B. Security Training

P.O. Box 697

Avon, CT 06001

Telephone: 203-677-5936

Fax: 203-677-9635

### Lockmasters Security Management

Lockmasters provides one- and two-day seminars in cities throughout the United States on topics such as controlling workplace violence, high threat security surveys, basic crime prevention, and theft control.

Contact information:

Lockmasters Security Management

5085 Danville Road

Nicholasville, KY 40356-9531

Telephone: 1-800-654-0637

Fax: 606-887-0810

## PRODUCTS

The following sources produce videotapes, audiotapes, publications, and other materials that may be useful to trainers.

### American Management Association

This organization offers a catalog of audio and videotapes for business trainers. See listing under Associations for contact information.

### American Society for Industrial Security

The ASIS O P Norton Resource Center provides not only books, but also video and audiotapes for free loan to members. This can be a great resource for trainers. See listing under Associations for contact information.

### Crisis Prevention Institute

In addition to training courses, CPI offers videotapes and posters of use to trainers teaching nonviolent crisis intervention techniques. See listing under Schools and Training Programs for contact information.

### Professional Security Television Network

This group provides high-quality videotapes on a wide variety of general and specific security topics. Videotapes not only cover relevant security topics, but also present updates and news about the industry. "It's your call" segments provide trainees with a scenario and ask them to determine the best possible response.

Contact information:

Professional Security Television Network

1303 Marsh Lane

Carrollton, TX 75006-9977

### Trainer's Advantage

A wide range of materials for trainers is available, including video tapes, audiotapes, workbooks, and self-paced programs. Topics include presentation skills, team building, and supervisor training.

Contact information:

Trainer's Advantage

4900 University Avenue

West Des Moines, IA 50266-6769

Telephone: 1-800-548-7304

Fax: 515-327-2527

## CareerTrack

CareerTrack offers videotapes, audiotapes, and seminars on many of the same types of subjects as Trainer's Advantage.

Contact information:

CareerTrack

MS2, 3085 Center Green Drive

Boulder, CO 80301-5408

Telephone: 1-800-488-0929

Fax: 1-800-832-9489

Web site: http://www.careertrack.com

## Calibre Press, Inc.

Calibre provides videotapes and books for law enforcement and the security industry and also conducts street survival seminars in cities around the United States. The emphasis is more law enforcement than security, but some products may be of value to security practitioners performing armed, high-risk or quasi-law enforcement duties.

Contact information:

Calibre Press, Inc.

666 Dundalk Road, Suite 1607

Northbrook, IL 60062-2760

Telephone: 1-800-323-0037

Fax: 847-498-6869

Web site: http://www.calibrepress.com

## MAGAZINES, NEWSLETTERS, AND OTHER PUBLICATIONS

Most professional organizations publish a magazine and/or newsletter. The only listing that appears twice here is for *Security Management* magazine. All other association publications are listed under their respective organizations.

### Security Management

Published by ASIS, *Security Management* is one of the best sources available in the field. Subscriptions are automatic with ASIS membership and are available to nonmembers for a fee.

Contact information:

*Security Management*

American Society for Industrial Security

1625 Prince Street

Alexandria, VA 22314

Telephone: 703-519-6200

Fax: 703-519-6299

Web site: http://www.securitymanagement.com

### Security

The focus is more technical than in *Security Management*, but it does cover some management and training issues and industry trends.

Contact information:

*Security*

1350 E. Touhy Avenue

P.O. Box 5080

Des Plaines, IL 60018

Telephone: 847-635-8800

Web site: http://www.secmag.com

## Security Technology & Design

As the name implies, this magazine has a technical focus. Articles and columns addressing training, security management, and consulting are included.

Contact information:

*Security Technology & Design*

850 Busse Highway

Park Ridge, IL 60068

Telephone: 847-692-5940

Fax: 847-692-4604

Web site: http://www.simon-net.com

## Security Letter

This newsletter covering the security industry has been in publication since 1970.

Contact information:

*Security Letter*

166 East 96th Street

New York, NY 10128

Telephone: 212-348-1553

Fax: 212-534-2957

## Security Law Newsletter

This newsletter covers case law and legal developments in the security industry.

Contact information:

*Security Law Newsletter*

1063 Thomas Jefferson St. NW

Washington, DC 20007

Telephone: 202-337-2700

Fax: 202-337-8324

## Security Director's Report

Published by the institute of Management and Administration, this publication covers developments in the security field.

Contact information:

*Security Director's Report*

29 West 35th Street

New York, NY 10001-2299

Telephone: 212-244-0360

Fax: 212-564-0456

Web site: http://www.ioma.com

## Security and Special Police Legal Update

This provides case law summaries relevant to security. The summaries are arranged by topic.

Contact information:

*AELE Security Legal Update*

P.O. Box 75401

Chicago, IL 60675-5401

Telephone: 1-800-763-2802

Fax: 1-800-763-3221

### Security Management Bulletin

This newsletter covers updates and trends within the security industry.

Contact information:

*Security Management Bulletin*

Bureau of Business Practice

24 Rope Ferry Road

Waterford, CT 06386

Telephone: 1-800-876-9105

Web site: http://www.bbpnews.com

## WEB SITES

These web sites may be useful to security trainers. Most of the resources listed already in this chapter also have web sites; these are not posted twice.

### Terrorism Research Center

This site provides information regarding terrorist incidents and terrorist groups.

http://www.terrorism.com

### Contingency Planning and Management

Information on emergency management and business continuity is available at this site.

> http://www.contingencyplanning.com

### Security Professional's Web Site

This site contains a list of links to various related security sites.

> http://www.freeyellow.com/É/index.html

### Security Academy

This web site provides information about security and a list of links to various web sites of interest.

> http://www.goodnet.com/~ej59217/

### NACJ Criminal Justice Page

A list of links of interest to the security practitioner is available at this site.

> http://www.nacj.com/links/mega.htm

### EmergencyNet News Today!

This content-rich web page contains news and information for security and emergency response professionals.

> http://www.emergency.com/ennday.htm

# Appendix A
## XYZ CORPORATION ORIENTATION MANUAL FOR SECURITY PERSONNEL

## LOCATION

The headquarters of XYZ Corporation is located at 323 Main Street in the downtown business district. There are branch business offices located in fifteen U.S. cities and seven foreign countries. All security personnel are based at the corporate headquarters, but can be assigned as a temporary duty to any of the U.S. or foreign locations for a period of up to forty-five days, if required.

## PHYSICAL DESCRIPTION OF BUILDING

XYZ headquarters building, also known as the XYZ building, is a twenty-five story commercial office building. XYZ Corporation owns the building and occupies all of the floors; there are no other tenants.

151

## ACCESS CONTROL

XYZ uses picture ID to screen access to the building elevator banks. A card access system is used to control access on individual floors. Refer to the Security Manual for more detailed information regarding access control procedures.

## SECURITY DEPARTMENT MISSION

The mission of the security department is to protect the employees and physical and intellectual assets of XYZ Corporation.

## SECURITY DEPARTMENT ORGANIZATION

The security department is located on the fourth floor/east wing.
   The security department is composed of the following:

- Administrative Section
- Uniformed Guard Force
- Investigative Group
- Executive Protection Section
- Technical Section
- Information/MIS Liaison Group

   For a more detailed description of the security department organization and contact numbers, refer to the Security Procedures Manual.

## SECURITY DEPARTMENT FUNCTIONS

- Physical security of XYZ Corporation facilities and property
- Emergency response activities

- Investigations regarding violations of company policy, thefts of company property and other incidents
- Development of programs to reduce risk
- Threat assessment and mitigation
- Security support to branch offices and external activities
- Personal protection for CEO and other executive staff
- Security awareness programs for employees
- Information security program/MIS liaison program
- Law enforcement liaison

## UNIFORMED SECURITY FORCE POSTS

| POST NUMBER | DESCRIPTION |
| --- | --- |
| 1 | Main Lobby Entrance Security Post |
| 2 | Main Lobby Reception Desk |
| 3 | A & B Elevator Banks |
| 4 | C & D Elevator Banks |
| 5 | Shipping & Receiving/Freight Entrance |
| 6 | East Vehicle Gate |
| 7 | West Vehicle Gate |
| 8 | Roving Patrol |
| 9 | Roving Patrol |
| Console | Console Operator |
| Supervisor | Shift Supervisor |

## RADIO USAGE

Each member of the uniformed security force is equipped with a portable radio. Radio transmissions should be brief and to the point. More detailed information should be passed by telephone ("land-line"). Radio volume should be kept at a level where it can be understood, but which does not create a disturbance, particularly when traveling through company workspaces.

## RADIO CODES

| CODE | MEANING |
| --- | --- |
| 10–1 | Report to console |
| 10–2 | Call console on the telephone |
| 10–3 | Report to (name location) |
| 10–4 | Acknowledge—"I understand" |
| 10–5 | Say again—repeat your transmission |
| 10–6 | Communication check |
| 10–7 | Meal break |
| 10–8 | Smoke condition |
| 10–9 | Fire |
| 10–13 | Emergency situation—need immediate help |
| 10–20 | Location |

## KEY PERSONNEL

It is critically important that all members of the security department, even new members, know the names and titles of key personnel within XYZ Corporation.

| | |
| --- | --- |
| Chief Executive Officer: | James Michaelson |
| Chief Financial Officer: | Lawrence Abbot |
| Chief Operations Officer: | Shirley McNeil |
| Chief Information Officer: | Andrew Martins |
| Senior VP Operations: | Dick Harcourt |
| Senior VP Sales: | Madeline Richards |
| Senior VP Facilities: | James Dawson |
| Asst. Director Facilities: | Michelle Hewitt |
| Director Human Resources: | Antoinette Carson |
| Director of Security: | Joseph Williams |
| Asst. Director of Security: | Peter Harris |
| Director of Management Information Systems: | Herbert Osgood |
| Director of Telecommunications: | Mary Fine |

Corporate Counsel:                                    Harvey Osborn
Building Maintenance Manager:                         Larry Halliday
Mailroom/Reproduction Center Manager:                 Sebastian Samuels

## CONTACT INFORMATION

The following contact phone numbers have been provided to give security department personnel ready access to key telephone extensions. For additional company telephone extensions, refer to the XYZ Corporation telephone directory. For telephone numbers for outside contractors and service personnel, refer to the Security Procedures Manual.

| DEPARTMENT | CONTACT PERSON | TELEPHONE EXTENSION |
|---|---|---|
| Security Department Office | Ann Chandler | 3235 |
| Security Console | Duty Console Operator | 3230 |
| Front Gate Security Post | Duty Security Officer | 3231 |
| Lobby Security Post | Duty Security Officer | 3232 |
| Lobby Reception Desk | Duty Security Receptionist | 3233 |
| Human Resources | Karen Wildwood | 3669 |
| Facilities | Joseph Casey | 4322 |
| Building Maintenance | Larry Halliday | 4327 |
| Information Systems | Miles Stanfords | 4302 |
| Telecommunications | Harriet Miller | 3739 |
| Finance | Stephen Purchase | 4333 |
| Mailroom | Sebastian Samuels | 4166 |
| Executive Floor Receptionist | Annette O'Rourke | 5212 |
| Nurse | Shelly Myers | 4168 |
| Cafeteria | Sandy Nelson | 0021 |
| Shipping & Receiving | Paul DeMichelle | 0031 |

## TRAINING

As a member of the security department at XYZ Corporation you will receive initial classroom instruction on the following topics:

1. Company Security Policies Overview
2. Access Control Procedures
3. Property Removal Procedures
4. Emergency Response
5. Public Relations
6. Report Writing

Following this classroom instruction, members of the uniformed security force will be given on-site orientation training. Security specialists will be trained in their respective skills by the group to which they are assigned.

On-site training for the uniformed security force members will consist of forty hours of post-oriented training interspersed with occasional lectures from the security trainer.

Following the orientation training period, the trainee will be paired with a more experienced staff member for three to five days of double posting.

Training will be ongoing after the new member has completed initial training. Drills, practical exercises, and special skills training will be held continually to improve the security force's ability to function effectively.

## ORIENTATION FOR SECURITY STAFF

| Subject/Post | Number of Hours | Date of Training | Initials of Trainee | Initials of Trainer |
|---|---|---|---|---|
| Access Control | 2 | | | |
| Emergency Response | 2 | | | |

*Continued*

| Subject/Post | Number of Hours | Date of Training | Initials of Trainee | Initials of Trainer |
|---|---|---|---|---|
| Legal Powers | ? | | | |
| Report Writing | 1 | | | |
| Public Relations | 1 | | | |
| Ethics and Conduct | 1 | | | |
| Post 1 Main Lobby | 7 | | | |
| Post 2 Reception | 6 | | | |
| Post 3 Freight | 4 | | | |
| Post 4 Floor Patrol | 6 | | | |
| Post 5 Perimeter Patrol | 4 | | | |
| Post 6 Relief/ Response | 4 | | | |
| Total Hours | 40 | | | |

## STACKING PLAN FOR XYZ CORPORATE HEADQUARTERS AT 323 MAIN STREET

| FLOOR | DESCRIPTION |
|---|---|
| 25 | Executive Offices/Dining Room |
| 24 | Executive Offices/Conference Rooms |
| 23 | Corporate Finance |
| 22 | Cafeteria |
| 21 | Legal Department |
| 20 | Global Operations |
| 19 | Global Operations |
| 18 | Technology Division |
| 17 | Support Services |
| 16 | North American Operations |
| 15 | North American Operations |
| 14 | North American Operations |
| 13 | Office Services/MIS |

*Continued*

| FLOOR | DESCRIPTION |
|-------|-------------|
| 12 | Global Sales & Marketing |
| 11 | North American Sales & Marketing |
| 10 | Marketing/Public Relations |
| 9 | Office Services/Facilities |
| 8 | Mailroom/Copy Center |
| 7 | MIS |
| 6 | MIS |
| 5 | Accounting/MIS |
| 4 | Accounting |
| 3 | Corporate Travel |
| 2 | Human Resources |
| Lobby | Reception Desk/Food Delivery Area |
| B-1 | Building Engineering |
| B-2 | Storage/Parking |
| B-3 | Storage/Parking |

# Appendix B
## *Sample Security Operations/Procedures Manual*

The sample security manual in Appendix B is typical of the type of manual that should be used by the instructor conducting practical training. Clearly, the manual's intended purpose is use by the security personnel as a guideline for conducting their duties. It does, however, serve the additional purpose of acting as an outline and a measuring stick for the trainer to develop a functional, practical program. The procedures depicted in the manual are designed for use at the fictional XYZ Company; they may or may not be applicable to the reader's organization.

This sample manual is intentionally a very "bare-bones" model. As XYZ is a fictional organization, this manual does not reflect any of the company character or philosophy that would typically be found in a real organization's manual. Likewise, the post and emergency procedures are very basic. In reality, the manual would give more extensive direction in these areas.

XYZ CORPORATION SECURITY OPERATIONS MANUAL
Confidential—For use by XYZ Security Department Personnel
Do Not Copy—Do Not Remove from Premises

## TABLE OF CONTENTS

## SECTION I: INTRODUCTION

The security operations manual was created to provide a standard set of guidelines and procedures for XYZ security department personnel. Every effort has been made to keep this document as current as possible. Any inconsistencies or omissions should be brought to the attention of security management for correction.

All XYZ security department personnel are responsible for their own familiarity with the contents of this manual. Knowledge of these procedures will better enable security personnel to carry out their assigned tasks in a professional manner.

This manual is a confidential document. Its contents should not be copied, removed from the premises, or disseminated in any way.

## SECTION II: SECURITY POSTS

Post 1: Main lobby entrance security post

Post 2: Main lobby reception desk

Post 3: A & B elevator banks

Post 4: C & D elevator banks

Post 5: Shipping in receiving/freight entrance

Post 6: East vehicle gate

Post 7: West vehicle gate

Post 8: Roving patrol

Post 9: Roving patrol

Console: Console operator

## SECTION III: EMERGENCY CONTACT INFORMATION

| | |
|---|---|
| Police department | 911 |
| Fire department | 911 |
| Emergency medical services | 911 |
| Security console | 3230 |
| Security department office | 3235 |
| MEDEX Ambulance Service | 321–7175 |
| Building maintenance | 4327 |
| Nurse | 4168 |
| Glazier | 471–3234 |
| Electrician | 471–6843 |
| Plumber | 584–2790 |

## SECTION IV: GENERAL SECURITY PROCEDURES

### Access Control

For the safety of all its employees, XYZ Corporation has established strict policies regarding access control for the company facilities. All company employees must present a valid ID card when entering company property. Employees who have lost or forgotten their ID card must report to visitor reception and be issued a visitor pass. This pass can only be issued with the approval of the employee's department manager.

All visitors must be announced or preapproved to enter the building. Visitors will report to visitor reception and be issued a pass.

Contractors and temporary employees will be issued special identification or special passes depending on the duration of their work on company property.

Former employees must receive a visitor pass before being granted admission to the building. If a former employee is listed as nondesirable, authorization must be received from the security department before admittance is granted.

Messengers and other couriers will be directed to the shipping and receiving department where packages will be received and processed. Messengers and couriers are not permitted to enter the work spaces at corporate headquarters.

XYZ Corporation reserves the right to refuse entrance to anyone, including spouses and family members of employees if deemed necessary by the security department. This policy is in place to help ensure the safety of all employees.

If security personnel encounter employees or others in restricted areas or within the office spaces at unusual times, they have the right to request that the employee or other person display valid identification.

## *Property Removal*

Company policy requires that all personnel removing items from the workplace must have a property pass signed by an authorized signatory. Lists of authorized signatories and copies of their signatures can be found in the rear of this book. Property passes must be completed in their entirety and if computer or other electronic equipment is involved a serial for each item must be recorded on the pass. This serial number must match the equipment being removed. Persons failing to display an authorized property pass will not be permitted to remove property from the company premises.

Questions or disputes about property removal should be referred to the security console. Security personnel should be alert to the risk of persons stealing company property under the guise of removing it with a property pass. For this reason, a thorough check must be made of the property being removed and the signature on the property pass must match the signature in the authorized signatory list.

## General Patrol Procedures

Security personnel assigned to patrol duties should check the company area for safety hazards, possible criminal threats, potential fire hazards, and general maintenance and housekeeping problems. Security personnel conducting patrols must be very vigilant and aware of their surroundings. Any discrepancies should be reported to the security console upon completion of patrol. Security personnel should vary the times and routes of their patrols.

## Emergency Response Procedures

A separate section of this manual discusses responses to various types of emergency situations. In many cases the security officer on duty will be the first person on the scene and will have to take charge and manage the situation until public agency responders have arrived. In this regard, the security officer must have a good understanding of the proper procedures for many of these situations.

## Public Relations Duties

The security personnel form the first point of contact for many visitors to the company. Good public relations skills are essential in this regard. Security personnel must do everything in their power to enhance the professional image of XYZ Corporation. Another section of this manual discusses security department regulations, which will cover such areas as grooming, uniform maintenance, personal hygiene, and general standards of conduct and behavior.

## Communications

Each member of the security force is equipped with a portable radio. This radio is to be used for communication with the security console and other members of the security force. Each member of the security staff will receive training in portable radio usage. It is vitally important that the radio be used in a professional manner at all times. Transmissions should be kept as brief as possible and radio codes should be used to enhance brevity. More detailed information can be passed by telephone, also referred to as a *land line*. Confidential information should not be passed on the portable radio. Radio volume should be kept low, particularly when passing through office spaces. Security personnel are responsible for being familiar with the following radio codes:

| CODE | MEANING |
| --- | --- |
| 10–1 | Report to console |
| 10–2 | Call console on the telephone |
| 10–3 | Report to (name location) |
| 10–4 | Acknowledge: "I understand" |
| 10–5 | Say again: Repeat your transmission |
| 10–6 | Communication check |
| 10–7 | Meal break |
| 10–8 | Smoke condition |
| 10–9 | Fire |
| 10–13 | Emergency situation: Need immediate help |
| 10–20 | Location |

All security staff members must be proficient in the use of the company telephone system. When assigned to a post with a telephone, the security officer should answer all incoming phone calls as follows: "Good morning (afternoon, evening) Post ___, security officer _____ speaking. How may I help you?"

When taking a message, always ask for the caller's name and a number where they can be contacted. All security personnel should be familiar with how to transfer phone calls and set up conference calls.

All security personnel are reminded that the telephones on company property are for company business only. Disciplinary action will be taken against personnel who abuse their access to company telephones.

### Report Writing

Report writing is an essential skill that must be mastered by all members of the security staff. Security department reports may be used for insurance purposes, introduced as evidence at civil and criminal court proceedings, and used during quality-control evaluations. For these reasons, every member of the security staff must strive to write clear, concise, effective reports.

Report writing skills apply not only when completing incident reports, but also when making log book entries or completing other forms of documentation. Security personnel should follow the following guidelines when writing reports:

- Be clear and concise
- Use good spelling and grammar
- Be objective
- Avoid jargon and acronyms
- Describe events in logical order
- The report must be clear to an outsider with no prior knowledge of the incident

Security personnel should endeavor to answer the following questions in their report:

- Who?
- What?
- Where?
- When?
- Why?

When in doubt about the quality of a report, the report should be submitted to the shift supervisor for review before being officially submitted.

## SECTION V: POST PROCEDURES

This section gives a brief outline of the security posts at corporate headquarters. Every member of the security force will receive training on these posts.

### Post 1: Main Lobby Entrance

The security officer assigned to Post 1 will observe individuals as they enter the building and direct them to the appropriate location. For example, visitors will be directed to the main lobby reception desk. This security officer will greet company employees as they enter the building. This security officer will also be responsible for challenging people who appear not to be employees of the Corporation. This post is manned 24 hours a day, seven days a week.

### Post 2: Main Lobby Reception Desk

The security officer assigned to the main lobby reception desk will be responsible for screening visitors and employees without an ID card. This security officer will call to announce visitors and will be responsible for issuing passes. This post is manned from 7:30 A.M. to 5:30 P.M.

### Post 3: A and B Elevator Banks

This security officer will be responsible for checking ID cards and passes before allowing admittance to the elevator bank. The security officer will likewise check all property passes as people leave the elevator bank. This post is staffed 24 hours a day, seven days a week.

### Post 4: C and D Elevator Banks

Procedures are the same as Post 3.

### Post 5: Shipping and Receiving/Freight Entrance

The security officer assigned to Post 5 will be responsible for screening all deliveries that enter the building. Actual processing of the deliveries will be conducted by shipping and receiving personnel. However, this security officer will be responsible to oversee the screening of all delivery personnel prior to their entering the building. This security officer will be responsible for notifying key department people regarding deliveries for their sections. The security officer will also be responsible for monitoring the egress of personnel through the freight area and verifying property passes before allowing property to be removed. This post is staffed from 7 A.M. to 6 P.M.

## Post 6: East Vehicle Gate

The officer at this post will be responsible for screening all service vehicles entering company property. The security officer will ensure that the delivery is approved prior to granting access. This security officer will also inspect departing vehicles to ensure that no property is being inappropriately removed. This post is staffed from 7 A.M. to 7 P.M., Monday through Friday.

## Post 7: West Vehicle Gate

The officer at this post will be responsible for screening all employee vehicles entering company property. The security officer will ensure that all vehicles have a valid sticker prior to granting access. This post is staffed 24 hours a day, seven days a week.

## Post 8: Roving Patrol

This security officer will be responsible for patrolling the perimeter and exterior grounds of the company property. The patrol officer is to be on the lookout for any potential hazard or danger that may exist. This would include suspicious items, unusual activity, and perimeter vulnerabilities. This post is staffed 24 hours a day, seven days a week.

## Post 9: Roving Patrol

This security officer patrols the interior floors. The security officer focuses on noticing potential hazards and problems, and responding to incidents as directed by the security console. This post is staffed 24 hours a day, seven days a week.

### Console Operator

The console operator reports directly to the shift supervisor. The console operator is responsible for the deployment of the security force, post assignments, meal breaks, coordinating emergency response, and monitoring a proprietary station alarm system and CCTV system. This post is staffed 24 hours a day, seven days a week.

## SECTION VI: EMERGENCY RESPONSE PROCEDURES

### Fire

These tasks normally are done by the console operator.

1. Notify fire department
2. Alert employees in affected area to alarm condition
3. Mobilize fire response team
4. Prepare to evacuate affected areas
5. Notify security department management
6. Dispatch security team member to make liaison with fire department

### Medical Emergency

These tasks normally are done by the console operator.

1. Notify emergency medical services
2. Dispatch security team member to safeguard the victim and administer first-aid as required
3. Dispatch staff member to make liaison with the ambulance and escort them to the victim
4. Place one elevator on "attendant service" to expedite response

5. Gather all pertinent information on the victim for reporting purposes
6. Notify security department management

### Bomb Threat

1. Copy all information from the caller; utilize bomb threat checklist if available
2. Notify security department management
3. Notify police
4. Begin a search of designated areas
5. Treat any suspicious item using the procedures for suspect items

### Suspect Item Procedures

1. A suspect item may be found as part of the search following a bomb threat or independent of a bomb threat; procedures for dealing with the item are the same in either situation
2. Do not touch a suspect item or move it in any way
3. Isolate the suspect item by approximately 300 feet (situation dependent)
4. Notify police
5. Do not use radios in the vicinity of a suspect item as radio signals may cause an explosive device to detonate

### Elevator Entrapment

1. When receiving an elevator alarm, make contact with the occupants in the elevator
2. Ensure that elevator occupants are safe
3. Notify elevator mechanics immediately
4. Remain in contact with elevator occupants throughout the entrapment; advise them that help is on the way

### Civil Disturbance

1. When a civil disturbance occurs in the vicinity of the property, the security force should concentrate on protection of company property and employees

2. All the secondary entrances and exits should be secured and the security force massed at the main entrance
3. All shift reliefs will be suspended for the duration of the crisis
4. Observers will be posted to view activity in the vicinity of the company property

## Power Outage

1. In the event of power outage during working hours, the security force will follow the procedures for a building evacuation
2. Security department management, facilities, and maintenance management should all be notified immediately
3. In the event of a power outage during nonworking hours, the security force will evacuate employees within the building and will deny access to others for the duration of the outage
4. Special attention should be given to ensure that there is no theft or vandalism during the power outage
5. Due to the risk of elevator entrapment, all elevators should be checked during the evacuation and, if necessary, elevator mechanics notified to free entrapped occupants

## Building Evacuation

1. In the event an evacuation of all or part of the building is deemed necessary due to fire, natural disaster, structural damage, or other reason, the building will be split into quadrants and several floors in each quadrant evacuated simultaneously
   Quadrant 1: floors 25–19
   Quadrant 2: floors 18–13
   Quadrant 3: floors 12–7
   Quadrant 4: floors 6–B3
2. Employees should be notified about the evacuation through use of the building public address system
3. Two floors per quadrant may be evacuated at one time

4. Employees are to be instructed to use the stairs, not the elevators

5. Two members of the security staff will be assigned to each quadrant to assist in supervising the evacuation

6. Medi-chair equipment is available for evacuating physically challenged employees

7. Floor fire wardens will administer the evacuation on each floor under the supervision of the security staff

## SECTION VII: SECURITY DEPARTMENT REGULATIONS

The security department plays an important role within the company. In addition to protection duties, the security personnel play an important public relations function. Personal appearance is the key aspect of security's public relations function. All security personnel are to follow the following guidelines with regard to personal appearance and grooming:

1. Males will be clean-shaven or will wear a well-groomed beard or mustache. Razor stubble or five o'clock shadow is unacceptable.
2. Personnel will wear a clean uniform or business attire depending upon their duties.
3. Footwear will consist of suitable business shoes, which will be shined.

Punctuality and good attendance are key requirements of the security staff. Security personnel will be heavily evaluated on their ability to report to work in a timely manner and maintain good attendance. Personnel who will be absent due to sickness or personal emergency will notify the security console as early as possible, but no later than two hours before the start of their shift.

Security department personnel will conduct themselves in accordance with the highest standards of XYZ Corporation. Security personnel will refer to their employee handbook regarding standards of conduct for company employees. Due to the sensitive nature of the security department function, security staff members will be expected to perform to a higher standard than that expected of other employees.

# Appendix C
## *Additional Hypothetical Situations*

The following hypothetical situations have been included to assist security trainers with finding applicable scenarios for their training programs.

## THREATENING LETTER

An executive at XYZ Corporation receives a letter postmarked in a different state. The letter refers to a company policy that has been unpopular with environmental groups. While the letter is handwritten in a childish scrawl and appears disorganized, it refers to "severe consequences" if the policy is not discontinued. The bottom of the note has a drawing of a black bomb with a burning fuse. The letter is signed with the words "ka-boom."

1. What law enforcement/governmental agencies should be notified?
2. What steps should be taken to protect the executive who received the letter?
3. What sources should be used to gather intelligence about individuals or groups that may be responsible for the threat?

4. What security measures should be implemented or increased at the facility?

## SUSPICIOUS VEHICLE

A security officer making a perimeter patrol of the building after hours notices a vehicle circling the block. There are numerous parking spaces available, so it does not appear that the driver is looking for parking.

1. Who should the security officer notify?
2. What action should the security officer take regarding gathering information?
3. What possible threats could this vehicle constitute?

## SUSPICIOUS PERSON

The security officer working the concierge post notices a man loitering outside the building. The man is not creating a disturbance of any sort, but appears to be watching the comings and goings of the employees who work there. After several hours the security officer becomes concerned. The man is standing on a public sidewalk in front of the building.

1. Who should be notified?
2. Should the security officer approach the man to question his behavior?
3. What possible type of threat could the man constitute?
4. What other action should be taken?

## DIGRUNTLED EMPLOYEE

The security officer in the main lobby receives a call from the sixth floor. There is an employee causing a disturbance on the floor. When the security officer arrives on the sixth floor, he finds a man yelling in the hallway. The security officer approaches the man and asks him what the problem is. The man yells at him to go away. Another employee informs the security officer that the man is upset about a task that he was assigned by the department manager. The manager has locked himself in his office and was the caller who notified security about the disturbance. The security officer approaches the man a second time and asks him to calm down so the problem may be resolved. The man begins to back away and tells the security officer "don't come any closer!"

1. How should the security officer safely approach the man?
2. How much space should the security officer have between himself and the employee?
3. What should the security officer direct the other employees on the floor to do while he is trying to calm the disgruntled employee?
4. What kind of environmental weapons exist in the office that the security officer must be concerned about?

## SLIP AND FALL

A contractor working in the building slips while entering the freight entrance. The security officer responds to the scene and finds the contractor complaining about a sore back. As the security officer approaches the contractor the security officer detects the odor of alcohol. There are several other workers standing nearby.

1. What information does the security officer need to learn from the contractor himself?
2. Who else should the security officer speak to?
3. Write a report to explain this incident from the perspective of the security officer.

## INTERNAL INVESTIGATION: SEXUAL HARASSMENT ALLEGATIONS

The security manager is summoned to a meeting at the human resources department. At the meeting the security manager learns that a member of the security force is allegedly sexually harassing a female employee of the company. The alleged harassment has occurred primarily in the evenings when the female employee has worked late and the security officer has been assigned to floor patrol. The female employee also states that she has received two phone calls from the security officer at her home.

1. What initial background information should the security manager try to develop after the meeting concludes?
2. Who else should the security manager interview before arranging an interview with the security officer in question?
3. Describe the investigative plan the security manager should use when conducting this internal investigation.
4. Who else should be consulted during the investigation process?

## INTERNAL INVESTIGATION: COMPUTER EQUIPMENT THEFT

The security manager receives a report that computer equipment has been reported missing from several floors at the company headquarters. Upon interviewing the employees who were assigned the equipment, the security manager discovers that the items were last seen between seven and eight in the evening and were discovered missing between seven and nine in the morning.

1. What are some resources that the security manager could use to learn who had access to the floors where the thefts occurred during the time period in question?

2. Describe the investigative plan the security manager should use when investigating these thefts.
3. What steps could be taken to reduce the possibility of further thefts both during and after the investigation?

## FIRE

The supervisor on the evening shift receives an alarm on the building fire system. The alarm indicates smoke on the fifth floor. Moments later the supervisor receives several phone calls from employees on the fifth and sixth floors regarding smoke on the floors.

1. Who must the supervisor ensure is notified immediately?
2. What action should the supervisor take regarding employees located on those floors?
3. What preparatory steps must the supervisor take prior to the arrival of the fire department?
4. What is the role of the security supervisor when the fire department has arrived?

## PROCESS SERVER

The security officer working at the main reception desk receives a process server who wants to serve papers to an employee in the company regarding a personal matter. The security officer has instructions for dealing with process servers for the company but not those delivering papers to specific individuals. As the security officer attempts to locate a supervisor, the process server becomes impatient and begins stating that she is an officer of the court and cannot be detained.

1. What should the security officer do to calm the process server?
2. What are the company policies on dealing with persons serving legal papers to individuals on company property?

## EXTREME MEDICAL EMERGENCY

Two contractors are working on the exterior of the building when they fall into a ground-level plate glass window. Both are badly cut and bleeding heavily. One contractor appears to be unconscious. The second worker is conscious but exhibiting signs of shock. A security officer arrives at the scene after receiving reports about the noise of the broken window. The security officer sees the two injured workers lying on the ground.

1. What is the first action that should be taken?
2. What medical aid should the security officer administer immediately?
3. What possible hazards still exist to endanger the workers and the security officer?

## MEDIA INTERACTION

An electrical fire forces the evacuation of the corporate headquarters. Employees are evacuated to a rally point away from the building. As fire department personnel arrive to combat the fire, so do several news trucks. A reporter approaches the security officer posted outside the building and begins asking questions about the incident.

1. What should the security officer say about the incident?
2. To whom should inquiries be referred?
3. Should the security officer give any personal information to the reporter?
4. What should the security officer do if the reporter persists in asking questions?

## RECOVERED PROPERTY

A janitor reports to the security officer at the freight entrance that he has discovered two laptop computers in a bag among garbage bags near the freight elevator. The security officer notifies the console operator, who in turn notifies the security manager.

1. What should the security manager do first?
2. How can the security manager attempt to learn who placed the equipment in the garbage?
3. What resources can the manager and department investigators use in the investigation?
4. What other department should be contacted as part of the investigation?

## DISCOVERING DRUG PARAPHERNALIA

A security officer conducting an interior patrol discovers drug paraphernalia on an internal stairwell. The security officer reports it to the console operator. The console operator notes that other drug paraphernalia has been found in other remote parts of the building. In the other cases, the butts of marijuana cigarettes were found. As a result of these discoveries, there is reason to believe that there are several employees or contractors in the building using drugs. The console operator reports this to the security manager. The security manager elects to begin an investigation.

1. What should the security manager do first?
2. What methods can be used to learn the identity of the employees or contractors using drugs?
3. What can the security force do to discourage employees from abusing drugs, particularly in the workplace?

## DEALING WITH A VAGRANT

A security officer on perimeter patrol discovers a vagrant sleeping in the fire exit doorway in the front of the building. When the security officer tries to wake the vagrant, the individual becomes very agitated. The security officer explains that the building is private prop erty. The vagrant responds with something unintelligible and then begins to curse the security officer. The security officer again politely asks the vagrant to leave the premises, and again the vagrant curses the security officer and refuses to leave.

1. Who should the security officer contact first?
2. What threats should the security officer be cautious of?
3. What are some potential health hazards for the security officer?

## DEALING WITH AN EMPLOYEE ALTERCATION

The console operator on duty receives a phone call from the cafeteria reporting that two employees are fighting in the kitchen. The console operator dispatches two security officers to the kitchen of the cafeteria. Upon arriving on the scene, the two security officers find two employees fighting. One employee has cut the other with a cleaver and there is blood on the floor.

1. What should the security officers do upon arrival at the scene?
2. Who should be notified immediately?
3. Even if the altercation has ended, what health threat may exist for the security officers and others at the scene?

## RESPONDING TO A SEIZURE VICTIM

A security officer on duty in the lobby is notified by an employee that there is a person having a seizure on the second floor. The security officer notifies the console operator and then proceeds to the second floor with the employee. Upon arriving on the second floor, the security officer finds a person lying on the floor exhibiting signs of seizure activity. A group of coworkers is gathered around the person, who is thrashing back and forth on the floor.

1. What should the security officer do about the co-workers surrounding the seizure victim?
2. How can the security officer safeguard the victim during the seizure?
3. What information should the security officer attempt to gather to aid the emergency responders when they arrive?

# Appendix D
## *Additional Case Studies*

The case studies included in Appendix D represent some different types of security situations that may be of use to security trainers in training and developing both line personnel and security managers. These additional case studies are provided to give the reader additional situations that security professionals may confront. Many of the case studies included in this section are directed toward security management personnel or deal with crisis management situations. Following each case study are several questions for consideration. The trainer may choose to use these questions or develop additional questions based upon the case study.

### EMPLOYEE KIDNAPPED ABROAD

One classic case of a U.S. employee kidnapped overseas is the 1976 abduction of Beatrice Foods manager Gustavo Curtis. Curtis was the manager of the Colombian affiliate for Beatrice Foods. The Curtis case is very interesting, because it appears that he received warnings that he was a target, yet initially chose to ignore these. Officials at the U.S. Embassy in Bogota informed Curtis that they had discovered a surveillance photograph of him. When Curtis viewed the picture he claimed the subject in the picture was wearing a tie and jewelry that he did not own. Colleagues of Curtis advised him to leave the country immediately. At this point it appears Curtis began to take the situation seriously. He requested transfer from Beatrice Foods; this was apparently ignored or delayed.

On the evening of September 28, 1976, at approximately 7:30 P.M., as Gustavo Curtis was driving home from work along his usual route, his car was cut off on a narrow side street. Curtis was dragged from the car at gunpoint and put in another vehicle. Initially held for five million dollars in ransom, Curtis was released after eight months for a ransom of $465,000.

Despite having indications that Curtis was a target for kidnapping, Beatrice Foods took no action to safeguard him. Curtis was abducted while driving alone along the route he used every day at the same time.

Source: Auerbach, Ann Hagedorn. *Ransom.* Henry Holt and Company, New York, 1998, pp. 207–209.

1. What action could Curtis have taken on learning of the surveillance photo?
2. What could Beatrice Foods have done to enhance Curtis' personal security?
3. What simple action could Curtis have taken to reduce the chances of being ambushed and kidnapped?

## INDUSTRIAL ESPIONAGE

One of the growing concerns, particularly for companies in competitive industries, is the risk of economic or industrial espionage. One of the best tools that can be used to combat this threat is a good security awareness program. This case study illustrates how a company employee may be compromised into providing sensitive information to a competitor.

Karl Stohlze was an operative for the BND, Germany's foreign intelligence service. In 1989 Stohlze was in Boston to gather information on biochip development and production. Stohlze began his assignment by familiarizing himself with target companies in the

Boston area. Using social engineering skills, he was able to obtain a company telephone directory, and at that point he was off and running. Stohlze was able to get himself invited to a social function at the target company. While attending the party, he identified a female employee who seemed very shy and reserved. He focused on this woman and lavished her with charm. Through subsequent conversation Stohlze was able to determine that the woman had access to information about biochip development. In the days and weeks that followed the party, he pursued a romantic relationship with the woman.

The female employee was not normally inclined to share or steal information that would be of value to Stohlze. He eventually told the woman that he was having a problem at his job, which also involved biochip research. He told her that unless he produced significant results, he would be transferred back to Germany.

The woman quickly became afraid of losing someone who was so attentive and interested in her and she offered to do anything to help him. When he suggested that she bring him information on biochip research from her company, she was appalled. Stohlze immediately apologized. Two days later he told her he had a meeting in Washington, DC, which would determine his future. He then informed her that he would be transferred, probably back to Germany, in the very near future. At this time the woman volunteered to bring information from her company to him. Stohlze began to receive some material and treated her very well. He emphasized that he was pleased with this information, but that it was not sufficient to keep him in Boston. When she began to have second thoughts, he shifted to the blackmail approach. She began having to do more and more to gather information. This included making late-night visits to the office. It was during the course of these visits that she came to the attention of company security. While being interviewed in connection with the information theft, she requested to use the restroom and attempted suicide. Following this incident, she was taken to the company infirmary. She subsequently confessed to her part in the theft. At this time, however, Stohlze had already left the Boston area and was soon to leave the United States entirely.

Source: Winkler, Ira. *Corporate Espionage.* Prima Publishing, Rocklin, CA, 1997, pp. 229–238.

1. How could an effective security awareness program have defeated Stohlze's attempt to get the company phone directory?
2. How could an effective security awareness program have helped the woman when she first met Stohlze at the party?
3. Who should the woman have reported this meeting to?

## BOMBING ATTACK SUPPORTED BY DIVERSION

The New York City police department has officers permanently assigned to security outside the Cuban mission to the United Nations in Manhattan. On October 27, 1979, a man who appeared to be drunk and disorderly created a disturbance near the Cuban mission. Two police officers assigned to security of the mission left their posts to deal with the individual. Simultaneously, a violent explosion tore down part of the building's wall. The "drunk person" then proceeded to run away. It was later learned that the bomb was placed by Omega-7, a radical anti-Castro group.

Source: Mizell, Louis. *Target USA.* John Wiley & Sons, Inc., New York, 1998, p. 78.

1. How could the police officers have dealt with the "drunk" without compromising the security of the building?
2. What proactive steps could be taken to familiarize security personnel with the threat of diversionary tactics?

## CELEBRITY STALKING/ASSASSINATION

Rebecca Schaeffer, a young actress who starred in the television series *My Sister Sam*, was the victim of a deranged fan who stalked and

killed her. This incident has much to offer those who are responsible for security for high-profile people. The assassin, Robert Bardo, was a loner who had stalked other celebrities and studied the actions of other assassins like Mark Chapman (who killed John Lennon) and Arthur Jackson (who stabbed actress Theresa Saldana). Bardo sent letters to Schaeffer and in at least one case received a personal postcard in reply. The friendly nature of this postcard seemed to encourage Bardo further. Bardo used a private investigator to locate Schaeffer and arrived at her doorstep one Sunday morning. They spoke briefly and Bardo left. He returned a short while later and when she came to the door he shot her once in the chest, killing her. Bardo later spoke with protection and threat assessment expert Gavin DeBecker, who interviewed him in prison. Bardo told DeBecker that he had stalked other celebrities, but had not chosen them as a target due to the type of security they had. Bardo would use open source information, like print media, to learn if his target took security precautions or had bodyguards. This type of proactive action from the potential target tended to dissuade him from going any further.
Source: DeBecker, Gavin. *The Gift of Fear.* Little Brown and Company, New York, 1997, pp. 231–244.

1. What can security professionals learn about the value of deterrence from the Schaeffer case?
2. How could security awareness on the principal's part have led to a different result in this case?
3. What guidelines could be established for celebrities answering fan mail in the wake of this incident?

## WORKPLACE HOMICIDE

Michael Mantell and Steve Albrecht, the authors of *Ticking Bombs*, a respected book on workplace violence, use an excellent case study of a workplace homicide in their book. On January 24, 1992, Robert Mack, a long-time employee of General Dynamics in San Diego, California, shot and wounded his supervisor and shot and killed a labor relations representative. Mack had a history of absenteeism and lateness, which upset his supervisor, James English. As a result, Mack received a three-week unpaid suspension. Following the suspension, he received a termination letter in the mail. Mack was then summoned to a termination hearing. He armed himself with a .38 caliber pistol and went to the hearing. An argument erupted in the meeting between Mack and English and industrial relations representative Michael Konz. Mack then drew the weapon and killed Konz and seriously injured English. Mack later spoke at length with Steve Albrecht. During these conversation he detailed how he felt helpless and felt that the company was displaying no respect for him despite his many years of service. This frustration, combined with a feeling of loss of identity in losing his job, were two of the factors Mack told Albrecht led him to commit this act.

Source: Albrecht, Steve, and Mantrel, Michael. *Ticking Bombs*. Irwin Publishing, New York, 1994, pp. 93–134.

1. What are some suggestions that security could make to human resources and upper management to allow for safer terminations and reduce the risk of a workplace violence incident?
2. What type of physical security measures could have been used at the termination hearing that would have reduced the risk of this incident occurring?
3. What security measures other than physical security could have been used to reduce the tension and lessen the risk at the hearing?
4. How can managers and employees better identify the warning signs of a potentially violent worker?
5. How can these warning signs be used without using biased "profiling" methods that may create a liability for the company or constitute an unfair labor practice?

## INDUSTRIAL ESPIONAGE

Joe Elliot was a technician at a General Electric plant in Ohio. One night in May of 1989, Elliot received a call at home from a man identifying himself as Larry King of Sanyang Engineering Services. King displayed a great deal of knowledge about Joe and his work at GE. He told Joe that he was unappreciated and underpaid by GE, considering his experience and technical knowledge. King then offered Joe a chance to double his salary, get a $20,000 bonus, and other perks. The caller was actually Chien Ming Sung, a citizen of Taiwan who studied at Massachusetts Institute of Technology and had worked for GE on synthetic diamond projects. Sung was working for the Iljin Corporation, a South Korean manufacturing company, supplying them with information on producing diamonds. Sung needed someone to oversee the process and chose Elliot. Elliot contacted GE about the approach and they formed an investigative unit to explore the matter. Elliot and a GE investigator posing as his lawyer met with Sung and Iljin officials regarding a job opportunity. Sung was later uncovered and sued by GE and Norton, another company he had stolen secrets from.

Source: Schweizer, Peter. *Friendly Spies*. The Atlantic Monthly Press, New York, 1993, pp. 176–185.

1. What did Elliot do right?
2. How could the employer make its personnel aware of the possibility of recruitment by a competitor attempting to steal proprietary information?
3. How could companies better guard against people like Sung?

## ASSASSINATION BY AN EXTREMIST GROUP

Alan Berg was a vocal, combative and controversial talk radio personality in Denver, Colorado, in the early 1980s. Berg took pride in baiting Klansmen, Neo-Nazis, and other racists. Berg's inflammatory style and pride in being "the man you love to hate" brought him to the attention of the Order, an anti-Semitic white supremacist group in the Pacific Northwest. The leader of the Order was a man named Robert Matthews. Matthews was a charismatic leader who believed in white supremacy and sought to "remove the Jew forever from this world." Matthews was particularly incensed by a radio conversation between Berg and Roderick Elliott, the publisher of the *Primrose and Cattlemen's Gazette.* Berg invited Elliott on the show ostensibly because Rep. Patricia Schroeder of Colorado had accused the publication of being blatantly anti-Semitic and had forced Marine Corps recruiters to withdraw advertising from the publication. Berg claimed to support Elliott's First Amendment rights, but actually took the opportunity to ridicule Elliott's biased views.

Elliot eventually filed suit against Berg and his radio station, KOA, but the suit was dismissed a year later. The paper was finally forced to close, and the employees were laid off. One of the employees who lost his job was a former Klansman named David Lane. Lane later became involved with the Order. Around this time Matthews began to consider killing Berg. Matthews told Jean Craig, his girlfriend's mother and a middle-aged groupie of the Order, to travel to Denver and conduct a surveillance on Berg. Matthews said to Craig, "you know we've been knocking around the idea of having a talk with that radio guy in Denver, Alan Berg." For Matthews, "having a talk" was a euphemism for killing.

At the end of May 1984, Craig returned from the surveillance in Denver and gave her report to Matthews. Craig had visited the radio station in Denver and, posing as a journalism student, had requested information about Berg. She identified the vehicles he used: a black Volkswagen convertible and two others. She also learned the places he liked to eat dinner and discovered that his home address was listed in the telephone book. Berg's home was on a quiet street, and by monitoring his activity she learned that he usually came home at night. Matthews was very excited when he learned this information; he now had the background information necessary to plot an assassination.

Shortly after gathering this information, Matthews and David Lane set out for Denver. They stopped to see an associate in Fort Collins on the way, and when he asked why they were in the area, Lane replied "we're on our way to Denver for a business meeting."

Meanwhile, Alan Berg was following his standard routine. He awoke early and drove his black Volkswagen convertible to one of his favorite restaurants. Berg did his regular show at KOA in the morning and signed off at about 1 P.M. In the afternoon he drove to see clients for whom he did commercials in his spare time. He had plans that night to eat dinner with his ex-wife, Judith.

At 5:30 P.M. Berg met with his ex-wife. They chose a restaurant and went out to eat. At about 7 P.M., David Lane, Bob Matthews, and Bruce Pierce, another member of the Order, arrived on Adams Street, where Berg lived. Pierce had a MAC-10 submachine gun with a suppressor and 30-round magazine. At around 9 P.M., the three assassins saw Berg's Volkswagen turn down Adams Street. Berg slowed the car and then pulled away. The killers were dumbfounded; it appeared they had missed their opportunity. Had Berg seen the surveillance? In fact, Berg was merely tired and had decided to end the evening early. He drove Judith back to her car and then returned home. As his car turned up Adams Street, Lane started the killers' vehicle and pulled forward. Berg parked in his driveway and began to exit the car. Lane pulled across the opening to Berg's driveway and Bruce Pierce jumped out carrying the MAC-10. As Berg exited the car and stood up, he noticed Pierce. Pierce opened fire at point blank range, sending thirteen rounds into Berg's body and dropping him to the pavement. Pierce then bolted to the car and Lane sped away. A neighbor saw Berg's body and thought he had been mugged. The police were called and found him dead amid a pile of .45 caliber shell casings.

Source: Flynn, Kevin, and Gearhardt, Gary. *The Silent Brotherhood.* Signet, New York, 1989, pp. 209–250.

1. How could Berg have better protected himself?
2. What factor meant that the hit team would inevitably have located Berg, even if he had escaped that night?
3. What role would countersurveillance training have played in protecting Berg?
4. What resources could Berg have used to assess the threats against him?

# WORLD TRADE CENTER BOMBING

On Feb. 26, 1993 at 12:17 P.M. a 1500-pound bomb exploded in the World Trade Center in New York City. This explosion signaled the beginning of a new type of terrorism that would strike the United States at home. This incident is often considered the wake-up call for the U.S. security industry in terms of terrorism. Therefore, it is an important case to examine for security professionals designated with the protection of high-profile office buildings.

The bombers were a loose-knit group of Islamic extremists who followed the teachings of Sheikh Omar Abdel-Rahman, a blind Egyptian cleric who was the spiritual leader of Gama al-Islamiya, a radical Muslim fundamentalist group. The Sheikh was suspected of having a role in the assassination of Anwar Sadat, the late Egyptian president. The participants included Mahmoud Abouhalima, an "Arab-Afghan," one of the many Arabs who volunteered to fight with the Mujahadin guerillas against the Soviets in Afghanistan; Mohamed Salameh, a Jordanian who drove the van with the bomb; Nidal Ayyad, a Palestinian chemical engineer; and Ramzi Yousef, a professional terrorist and explosives expert.

The World Trade Center in New York City is a massive complex. It covers sixteen acres and is composed of seven buildings, the most notable being Towers 1 and 2. The Towers reach a quarter-mile into the sky. The complex houses 50,000 employees and another 80,000 people visit on a daily basis. The World Trade Center is administered by the Port Authority of New York and New Jersey. Security is provided by a contract security force and the Port Authority police. The complex also houses the New York offices of the U.S. Secret Service and the U.S. Customs Service. At the time of the bombing, a garage open for public parking existed within the complex. Since this incident, security has been significantly tightened, particularly with regard to vehicle parking.

Preparation for the bombing began in Jersey City, New Jersey. Jersey City, which is within eyesight of the World Trade Center, was the site of the bomb factory where the explosives that were detonated in the World Trade Center were made.

On the morning of February 26, the bombers set out for the World Trade Center in a caravan of three cars; the bomb had been loaded into a ten-foot Econoline van. The yellow van had been rented from a Ryder truck rental office in Jersey City and that morning was loaded with 1,500 pounds of explosives, including heavy hydrogen tanks to increase the effect of the bomb.

The Ford van entered the parking area of the World Trade Center and drove to B-2 level. This was not a public parking area, but was used by the vehicles of the Port Authority of New York and New Jersey. The yellow van blended in well with the yellow Port Authority vehicles. Using a lighter, the two men in the van ignited the four twenty-foot fuses. The fuses were encased in surgical tubing to suppress smoke and reduce the rate of burn and each fed to a separate Atlas Rockmaster blasting cap. They would take approximately twenty minutes to burn down. With the fuses lit, the two men quickly exited the parking area unobserved. As the van was parked in an illegal space, they had not passed through the toll gates for the paid-parking area.

The resulting explosion under Tower 1 killed six people and injured many more. While the terrorists' ultimate goal of toppling one tower into the other ultimately failed, it demonstrated the vulnerability of U.S. facilities and landmarks to international terrorism. The need for improved access control was somewhat addressed by more restrictive parking control, vehicle barriers, dogleg vehicle entrances, and increased personnel access control through the introduction of turnstile card access systems. However, the lack of threat awareness and security consciousness is still a serious problem. A major office complex a block from the World Trade Center still offers public parking and lax screening of incoming vehicles.

Source: Dwyer, Jim, Kocieniewski, David, Murphy, Deidre, Tyre, Peg. *Two Seconds Under the World.* Ballantine Books, New York, 1994, pp. 25, 26, 32, 194–196, 216–219.

1. What measures can be taken to reduce the risk of a vehicle bomb entering the internal parking area of a building?
2. What effect will this have on normal operations (delays, etc.)?

3. What is the role of an awareness program for security personnel in preventing this type of incident?
4. What is the role of an awareness program for nonsecurity personnel in preventing this type of incident?
5. What is the role of law enforcement liaison and how could preincident intelligence have helped to deter or mitigate this incident?

## OKLAHOMA CITY BOMBING

While the World Trade Center bombing may give security practitioners a good example of the danger of poor access control at internal parking garage entrances, the Oklahoma City bombing that devastated the Alfred P. Murrah Federal Building and claimed 168 lives demonstrated that the terrorist doesn't even need to get inside the facility or place the explosive inside the facility to do incredible damage. The bombing at the al Khobar Towers in Saudi Arabia and the bombings of the U.S. Embassies in Nairobi, Kenya, and Dar es Salaam, Tanzania, also illustrate this point.

In the Oklahoma City case, Timothy McVeigh and Mike Fortier visited every floor of the nine-story Alfred P. Murrah Federal Building prior to the attack. Posing as job seekers, they visited the offices of the Bureau of Alcohol, Tobacco, and Firearms, the Small Business Administration, and the IRS, as well as other federal agencies located there. They are also believed to have reconnoitered federal buildings in Phoenix, Arizona, and Omaha, Nebraska.

The plot to bomb the federal building is believed to have originated around September 13, 1994. Ammonium nitrate fertilizer for use in the bomb was purchased on September 30 and October 18 in McPherson, Kansas. On October 21, Timothy McVeigh purchased nitromethane racing fuel for $2,775 in Texas.

The reconnaissance of the Alfred P. Murrah Federal Building began around December 16. McVeigh and Fortier drove by and assessed it as a potential target. On April 14, 1995, McVeigh purchased a 1977 Mercury Marquis in Junction City, Kansas. He returned to Junction City and rented a twenty-foot Ryder truck on April 17, giving his name as Robert Kling and claiming to be traveling to Omaha, Nebraska. The bomb was then loaded on the rental truck. The bomb weighed about 4,800 pounds and was primarily composed of **ammonium** nitrate and fuel oil, commonly referred to as ANFO.

On the morning of April 19, McVeigh parked the Ryder truck outside the federal building. He activated the device and fled from the truck on foot. At 9:02 A.M. the bomb detonated, ripping into the structure twenty feet away with a pressure of almost 6,000 pounds per square inch. The outer facade of the building was fifty percent glass windows which, when struck by the shock wave, sent thousands of pounds of glass shrapnel flying into the building. The entire front of the building was sheared off; floor slabs fell, creating a pile of debris twenty-six feet deep. Over 6,000 cubic feet of soil was blown away, resulting in a crater eight feet deep and thirty feet wide. Because of the extent of the destruction, the remaining frame of the building was destroyed on May 23rd for safety reasons. On April 19 at 10:20 A.M., just a little over an hour after the bombing, McVeigh was arrested 78 miles north of Oklahoma City on Route 35. He was driving the 1977 Mercury Marquis he had purchased on April 14. The car had no license plate, which drew the attention of state trooper Charles Hanger.

The Oklahoma City bombing illustrates the threat that exists to buildings in the United States, both government and privately owned, from terrorist groups which are as likely to be domestic as foreign. Clearly, it is very difficult for security practitioners to prevent a situation like the Oklahoma City bombing. However, greater stand-off distances, more parking restrictions around large buildings, and greater awareness on the part of security staff may contribute significantly to reducing this type of threat. Another interesting facet of the Oklahoma City bombing was the symbolism of the date: April 19. April 19, 1993, was the date the Branch Davidian compound in Waco, Texas, burned to the ground. It was well known that McVeigh was furious at the federal government for the assault on the Branch Davidian compound and the resulting fire.

Sources: Gleick, Elizabeth. "Who are they?" *Time*, May 1, 1995, pp. 45–51.

Hinman, Eve E. "Lessons from Ground Zero." *Security Management*, October 5, 1995, pp. 26–35.

Murr, Andrew, Thomas, Evan, et al. "Inside the Plot." *Newsweek*, June 5, 1995, pp. 24–27.

——. "Bombing Time Line." *The Oklahoman*, archives, http://www.archives.oklahoman.com.

## DIVERSIONARY BOMB THREAT: OMAGH NORTHERN IRELAND

Whenever a bomb threat is received, it must be taken seriously. While this is common knowledge and may seem obvious, what is not always as obvious is the hidden danger that may be lurking behind the bomb threat. While it's true that approximately ninety-eight percent of bomb threats are hoaxes, it is very important to take every threat seriously. Sometimes the threat is real and sometimes the bomb threat is simply a diversion or a redirection for a more sinister act. The latter was the case on August 15, 1998, in the town of Omagh, Northern Ireland. It was the twenty-ninth anniversary of the deployment of British troops to Northern Ireland. Omagh is a small town of 20,000, west of Belfast, with a mixed population of Catholics and Protestants. On Saturday, August 15, the shopping area of Market Street and Dublin Road was crowded with people patronizing shops and running errands. A telephone bomb threat was phoned into the BBC office in Belfast, indicating that a bomb had been placed in the vicinity of the courthouse. The caller used recognized IRA code words when making the threat. Notified of the threat, the police began to clear the area around the courthouse, directing shoppers away from the perceived threat. Twenty minutes after the warning was received, a powerful car bomb, estimated to weigh about 500 pounds, exploded. The bomb did not explode at the courthouse, but rather in the area to which the people were being evacuated. The bomb killed twenty-eight people and injured over 200, some very seriously. An eighteen-month-old baby was killed and a pregnant woman had both of her legs blown off.

Suspicions quickly fell on an Irish Republican Army splinter group called the Real IRA. The Real IRA is led by a former quartermaster in the provisional IRA who broke with the leadership over support for the peace process. While the Real IRA is believed to be small, many of their members were formerly with the engineering department of the IRA. This engineering department is the section that makes bombs for terrorist attacks.

There are several elements of the Omagh bombing that should be of interest to security practitioners. Principally of importance is the clever way that the police were tricked into evacuating the shoppers directly into the kill zone. The bomb threat was placed with the deliberate intention of drawing more people into the blast area. Additionally, the attack occurred on a date that had significance for the terrorist group. Just as security practitioners must be alert for secondary devices when dealing with bomb incidents or potential bomb incidents, likewise, they must be aware of false or misleading threats that may draw them into a trap and inflict greater casualties.

Sources: Goldiner, Dave. "Car Bomb Kills 28 in N. Ireland." *New York Daily News*, Sunday, August 16, 1998 (from online archives).

EERI Watch Center. "Terrorist Bomb Kills 28 in Northern Ireland, 220 Hurt." *EERI Daily Intelligence Report*, EERI Risk Assessment Services, Sunday, August 16, 1998, http://www.emergency.com/omaghbmb.htm.

1. What considerations should be taken into account in view of the Omagh bombing when planning evacuation protocol, evacuation routes, and rally points?
2. How can security personnel better prepare to counter a deception operation like Omagh?
3. How can security personnel respond prudently to a bomb threat, without creating a situation in which evacuees are led into a kill zone?
4. What role does evacuation route reconnaissance and rally point inspection play when evacuating in response to a bomb threat?

## SARIN GAS ATTACK IN TOKYO

One of the greatest fears expressed by security practitioners in both the public and private sectors is the danger of a terrorist group possessing and using weapons of mass destruction (WMD). WMD refers to nuclear, chemical, and biological weapons that can inflict mass casualties. Many biological and chemical weapons are cheaper and easier to obtain than is popularly known. While many of these weapons are very sensitive and need optimal environmental conditions to be truly effective, the threat is real. The threat became a reality on March 20, 1995, in the subway system in Tokyo, Japan.

It was about 8:17 A.M. when toxic fumes were first reported in the Tokyo subway system. Some commuters collapsed and went into convulsions. Others fled the subway stations. The final casualty count was eleven dead, 5,500 injured. Two days later, Japanese police raided the headquarters of the Aum Shinri Kyo cult in Kamikuishiki and discovered chemicals used to make Sarin gas, a lethal nerve agent.

The Aum Shinri Kyo cult was formed in 1984 and took its present name in 1987. In 1989, the cult was granted official religious status, which in addition to a large tax break, gave the group a degree of immunity against government oversight. This immunity may have been a key factor in facilitating the group's activities that led up to the Sarin gas attack on the subways. The cult espoused beliefs that were a mix of Buddhism, Hinduism, and Christianity, combined with yoga and an adherence to the prophecies of Nostradamus.

The cult's leader was Shoko Asahara, a partially blind judo black belt and yoga teacher. Asahara owned a natural food store and sold herbal remedies prior to forming the cult. Asahara preached that he was the reincarnation of the Hindu god Shiva. Shiva is associated with violence and destruction, and much of Asahara's teachings dealt with prophecies of doom and the concept of Armageddon. In 1990, the cult attempted to break into politics by sponsoring candidates in parliamentary elections. Their candidates were soundly defeated, and this may have been the point where the cult adopted a more violent agenda.

The Aum Shinri Kyo grew to be a fairly large organization composed of 10,000 followers in Japan, 30,000 followers in Russia, and smaller chapters in the United States and Europe. Among Asahara's predictions was a war between Japan and the United States in 1997 and that a nuclear attack on Japan would kill all but one tenth of the population. Much of the cult's rhetoric was very anti-American. Documents seized by police indicate that the group had planned terrorist attacks on U.S. cities, notably New York, similar to the Tokyo subway attacks. Additional Aum Shinri Kyo writings discussed targeting Jews and cosmopolitan Japanese.

The Aum Shinri Kyo members used violence on several occasions prior to the subway attacks. In 1989, cult members kidnapped and murdered a Yokohama lawyer, Tsutsumi Yakamoto, and his family. On June 21, 1994, the cult released Sarin gas in the town of Matsumoto, which killed seven and injured 200.

On March 20, members of the cult placed wrapped packages on five subway cars on different train lines. In some cases the cult members worked in teams. As one train entered the station, the first member would place the Sarin container on the floor and the second would pierce it with an umbrella before they both fled. The first sign that a problem existed was when commuters began collapsing. Police and military chemical warfare experts responded to the scene, but not before eleven people were fatally overcome by the gas.

While the threat of chemical terrorism to a mass transit system is principally a concern for public safety officials, the private sector also needs to be aware of the threat from chemical and biological terrorism. One of the principle threats that is being considered by counterterrorism experts is the possibility that a chemical or biological agent may be introduced into the HVAC system of a large office building. If this were to occur during working hours, the potential for many casualties is very high. Knowledge of the existence of this threat may help security personnel to recognize the danger and take action more quickly, thereby saving lives. In some municipalities, public sector emergency response personnel are beginning to train for these scenarios. Opportunities may exist to host drills and simultaneously expose company security personnel to this training.

Sources: Quinn, John F. "Terrorism comes to Tokyo." http://www.asiaresearch.com/TerrorismTokyo.html.

Senate Government Affairs Permanent Subcommittee on Investigations. *A Case Study on the Aum Shinrikyo*, October 31, 1995.

New York State Department State Office of Fire Prevention and Control. *Emergency Response to Incidents Involving Nerve Agents, Biological Agents and Chemical Agents.* Draft 8/97, pp. 2, 4, 5.

1. What were some initial signs of the gas attack in the Tokyo subway?
2. How should a member of the security staff respond if people begin to faint or go into convulsions?
3. What description should be given to emergency services personnel prior to their entering the affected area?
4. What is the risk of people fleeing the contaminated area and leaving the property without being screened?
5. How should evacuees be safely controlled until emergency response personnel arrive?

## SIDNEY RESO KIDNAPPING

Corporate executives are an attractive target for kidnappers, whose goals may be political, financial, or both. By studying attacks on executives, security practitioners can better prepare to protect them and can educate them to protect themselves. The kidnapping of Sidney Reso, president of Exxon International, is an interesting example of the type of threat that exists. It is particularly interesting because it did not happen in an exotic, high-risk locale like Bogota, Colombia, but rather in suburban Morris Township, New Jersey.

Arthur Seal was a former police officer who worked in the security department at Exxon. In 1987 he left Exxon to start his own business. The business failed miserably and left Seal and his wife deeply in debt. Sometime around December 1991, the Seals determined that by kidnapping an Exxon executive for ransom, they could resolve their debt and still have money left. Seal began surveilling several Exxon executives to locate a suitable target. He ultimately chose Reso for several reasons. Reso was Exxon's president and often referred to as "Mr. Exxon," therefore his value to the company was well known. Reso's home was secluded and Seal considered him an easier target than many of the other executives. Despite his position, Reso led a relatively unpretentious life and declined the use of a security driver. After selecting Reso, Arthur Seal spent an additional four months conducting surveillance. On April 29, 1992, between 7:30 A.M. and 8:00 A.M., Reso drove down his long driveway to begin his trip to work. At his mailbox, he stopped to remove the newspaper, as he always did. Suddenly a van pulled in front of his car and Seal, wearing a ski mask, forced him from his car and into the van at gunpoint. At some point while forcing Reso into the van, Seal accidentally shot him in the arm.

Reso was then driven to a storage area that the Seals had rented in advance. Inside the storage locker they put Reso into a six-foot-four-inch by three-and-one-half-foot box with breathing holes. Reso was visited daily and fed vitamins and forced to make recorded messages. On day five of his captivity, he died. This did not prevent the Seals from sending a message to Exxon claiming to be from the Fernando Pereira Brigade of the Warriors of the Rainbow, a group allegedly linked to the Greenpeace environmental group. The kidnappers demanded an $18.5 million ransom.

The kidnappers were later arrested by police and Reso's body was discovered in June 1992. This case study is valuable because it illustrates that many of the tactics used by kidnappers are the same and that the greatest vulnerability is when the potential victim is traveling to and from work or performing other routine tasks.

Sources: "Scotti School on Kidnappings." *Scotti School WWW Newsletter*, http://www.ssdd.com.

Hagedorn Auerbach, Ann. *Ransom*. Henry Holt and Company, New York, 1998, pp. 224–225.

# Appendix E
## *Sample Evaluator Scenario Training Checklists*

Appendix E illustrates some example checklists that can be used by evaluators during any type of scenario-based training. The scenarios depicted on each checklist are very basic. The trainer may embellish or tailor the scenario as necessary. The participants can then be graded on their response. Comments may be included at the bottom of each checklist. Most scenarios that are presented are for line security officers, but some are designed specifically for supervisors and console operators.

## EVALUATOR CHECKLIST: INTRUDER SCENARIO

    Trainee: _____        Date: _____

    Evaluator: _____    Time: _____

The evaluator will grade the trainee on each of the following criteria. Indicate yes or no and circle the appropriate number regarding the trainee's response.

1 = Poor, 2 = Fair, 3 = Good, 4 = Very Good, 5 = Excellent

Scenario: A stranger attempts to bypass security and proceed upstairs without showing ID.

1. Security officer challenged the stranger and requested that ID be shown.
   ___ Yes ___ No     1    2    3    4    5
2. Security officer explained the access control policy to the stranger.
   ___ Yes ___ No     1    2    3    4    5
3. Security officer abandoned post to follow the intruder upstairs.
   ___ Yes ___ No
4. Security officer notified supervisor about the intruder.
   ___ Yes ___ No
5. Security officer shut down elevators to restrict intruder's movement.
   ___ Yes ___ No
6. Security officer notified police immediately.
   ___ Yes ___ No
7. Security officer completed incident report (grade quality of report).
   ___ Yes ___ No     1    2    3    4    5

# EVALUATOR CHECKLIST: PROPERTY REMOVAL

Trainee: ___ ___          Date: ___ ___
Evaluator: ___          Time: ___ ___

The evaluator will grade the trainee on each of the following criteria. Indicate yes or no and circle the appropriate number regarding the trainee's response.

1 = Poor, 2 = Fair, 3 = Good, 4 = Very Good, 5 = Excellent

Scenario: A person attempts to bypass security while carrying a mid-sized box.

1. Security officer challenged the person and requested that a property pass be shown.
   ___ Yes ___ No          1          2          3          4          5
2. Security officer explained the property removal policy to the stranger.
   ___ Yes ___ No          1          2          3          4          5
3. Security officer checked for a serial number if computer equipment was involved.
   ___ Yes ___ No
4. Security officer attempted to contact the person's manager.
   ___ Yes ___ No
5. Security officer notified supervisor about the person's failure to produce a pass.
   ___ Yes ___ No
6. Security officer requested the individual provide some form of identification.
   ___ Yes ___ No
7. Security officer completed incident report (grade quality of report).
   ___ Yes ___ No          1          2          3          4          5

## EVALUATOR CHECKLIST: TELEPHONE BOMB THREAT

Trainee: _____          Date: _____
Evaluator: _____        Time: _____

The evaluator will grade the trainee on each of the following criteria. Indicate yes or no and circle the appropriate number regarding the trainee's response.

1 = Poor, 2 = Fair, 3 = Good, 4 = Very Good, 5 = Excellent

Scenario: The security officer on duty receives a telephone call. The caller states that a bomb has been placed in the building and will explode.

1. Security officer remained calm and stayed on the phone with the caller.
   ___ Yes ___ No       1     2     3     4     5
2. Security officer copied the caller's words verbatim.
   ___ Yes ___ No       1     2     3     4     5
3. Security officer retrieved the bomb threat checklist and filled it out during the call.
   ___ Yes ___ No
4. Security officer notified supervisor immediately.
   ___ Yes ___ No
5. Security officer was able to describe caller's words accurately.
   ___ Yes ___ No       1     2     3     4     5
6. Security officer was able to describe caller's speech patterns, accent, approximate age, etc.
   ___ Yes ___ No       1     2     3     4     5
7. Security officer was able to describe background noises.
   ___ Yes ___ No       1     2     3     4     5
8. Security officer completed incident report (grade quality of report).
   ___ Yes ___ No       1     2     3     4     5

## EVALUATOR CHECKLIST: RESPONSE TO THEFT REPORT

Trainee: _____ Date: _____
Evaluator: _____ Time: _____

The evaluator will grade the trainee on each of the following criteria. Indicate yes or no and circle the appropriate number regarding the trainee's response.

1 = Poor, 2 = Fair, 3 = Good, 4 = Very Good, 5 = Excellent

Scenario: The security console operator on duty receives a telephone call from an employee reporting the apparent theft of a laptop computer. The console operator dispatches the trainee to take the report.

1. Security officer located the employee and explained that a report needed to be taken regarding the computer.
   ___ Yes ___ No
2. Security officer learned pertinent information about the computer that was believed stolen (make, model, serial number, employee issued to, etc.).
   ___ Yes ___ No      1      2      3      4      5
3. Security officer asked when computer was last seen and by whom.
   ___ Yes ___ No
4. Security officer asked who had access to area or was normally in that area at that time.
   ___ Yes ___ No
5. Security officer attempted to locate and interview other employees who work in that area.
   ___ Yes ___ No
6. Security officer determined a window of time when the theft probably occurred.
   ___ Yes ___ No
7. Security officer prepared incident report (grade quality of report).
   ___ Yes ___ No      1      2      3      4      5
8. Security officer recommended to console operator other assets to use (card access, CCTV, etc.) to determine activity in the area at the time in question.
   ___ Yes ___ No      1      2      3      4      5

## EVALUATOR CHECKLIST: RESPONSE TO MEDICAL EMERGENCY (CONSOLE OPERATOR)

Trainee: _____        Date: _____
Evaluator: _____      Time: _____

The evaluator will grade the trainee on each of the following criteria. Indicate yes or no and circle the appropriate number regarding the trainee's response.

1 = Poor, 2 = Fair, 3 = Good, 4 = Very Good, 5 = Excellent

Scenario: The security console operator on duty receives a telephone call from an employee reporting that another employee is suffering from chest pains.

1. The console operator gathered as much information as possible about the victim (name, age, symptoms, allergies, etc.).
   ___Yes ___ No      1      2      3      4      5
2. The console operator immediately notified 911 and requested an ambulance.
   ___Yes ___ No      1      2      3      4      5
3. Console operator dispatched a security officer to the floor to assist the victim.
   ___Yes ___ No
4. Console operator notified front lobby personnel of the situation (grade for clarity and completeness of instructions).
   ___Yes ___ No      1      2      3      4      5
5. Console operator designated elevator to be put on standby for use by the EMTs (grade for clarity and completeness of instructions).
   ___Yes ___ No      1      2      3      4      5
6. Console operator designated a security officer to meet the ambulance and escort the EMTs to the victim's location (grade for clarity and completeness of instructions).
   ___Yes ___ No      1      2      3      4      5
7. Console operator inquired to which hospital the victim would be taken.
   ___Yes ___ No
8. Console operator learned identities and badge numbers of EMT staff.
   ___Yes ___ No
9. Console operator ensured that security officers prepared incident report (grade quality of report).
   ___Yes ___ No      1      2      3      4      5
10. Console operator notified security manager of incident.
    ___Yes ___ No

## EVALUATOR CHECKLIST: SUSPECT ITEM RESPONSE (SECURITY OFFICER)

Trainee: _____     Date: _____
Evaluator: _____     Time: _____

The evaluator will grade the trainee on each of the following criteria. Indicate yes or no and circle the appropriate number regarding the trainee's response.

1 = Poor, 2 = Fair, 3 = Good, 4 = Very Good, 5 = Excellent

Scenario: The security officer, while patrolling the perimeter of the building, notices a blue knapsack on the ground against the side of the building.

1. The security officer attempted to locate the owner of the knapsack/determine if anyone in the area owned the knapsack.
   ___ Yes ___ No     1     2     3     4     5
2. The security officer asked anyone in the area (if applicable) if they saw who had placed the knapsack there or if anyone was loitering in the area.
   ___ Yes ___ No     1     2     3     4     5
3. Security officer turned off radio and reported knapsack to lobby personnel, instructing them to notify the console operator.
   ___ Yes ___ No     1     2     3     4     5
4. Security officer requested yellow caution tape to isolate knapsack.
   ___ Yes ___ No
5. Security officer did not touch, move, or disturb knapsack in any way.
   ___ Yes ___ No
6. Security officer isolated knapsack by 300 feet (approximately, situation-dependent).
   ___ Yes ___ No     1     2     3     4     5
7. Security officer awaited arrival of police, kept passersby from area.
   ___ Yes ___ No
8. Security officer completed incident report (grade quality of report).
   ___ Yes ___ No     1     2     3     4     5

## EVALUATOR CHECKLIST: SUSPECT ITEM
## RESPONSE (CONSOLE OPERATOR)

Trainee: _____      Date: _____
Evaluator: _____    Time: _____

The evaluator will grade the trainee on each of the following criteria. Indicate yes or no and circle the appropriate number regarding the trainee's response.

1 = Poor, 2 = Fair, 3 = Good, 4 = Very Good, 5 = Excellent

Scenario: The console operator receives a telephone message from the lobby security officer that the security officer patrolling the perimeter of the building has noticed a blue knapsack on the ground leaning against the side of the building.

1. The console operator asked if the security officer attempted to locate the owner of the knapsack/determine if anyone in the area owned the knapsack.
   __Yes __ No      1     2     3     4     5
2. The console operator notified the police and described the situation (grade quality and completeness of description).
   __Yes __ No      1     2     3     4     5
3. Console operator, via a messenger, notified all security personnel to turn off radios and use alternate means of communication (grade on clarity and completeness of instructions).
   __Yes __ No      1     2     3     4     5
4. Console operator dispatched yellow caution tape to security officer at site and directed that the knapsack be isolated (grade on clarity and completeness of instructions).
   __Yes __ No      1     2     3     4     5
5. Console operator dispatched security officer to make liaison with police and escort them to the site of the knapsack (grade on clarity and completeness of instructions).
   __Yes __ No      1     2     3     4     5
6. Console operator notified security manager of situation (grade on clarity and completeness of report).
   __Yes __ No      1     2     3     4     5
7. Console operator directed security officers to complete incident reports when situation was resolved (grade quality of report).
   __Yes __ No      1     2     3     4     5
8. Console operator completed incident report (grade quality of report).
   __Yes __ No      1     2     3     4     5

## EVALUATOR CHECKLIST: SUSPECT PACKAGE/ENVELOPE

Trainee: _____          Date: _____
Evaluator: _____          Time: _____

The evaluator will grade the trainee on each of the following crite ria. Indicate yes or no and circle the appropriate number regarding the trainee's response.

1 = Poor, 2 = Fair, 3 = Good, 4 = Very Good, 5 = Excellent

Scenario: The security officer is dispatched to the company mailroom in response to a report of a suspicious parcel that arrived through the mail.

1. The security officer questioned mailroom personnel as to what suspicious indicators were noticed on the parcel.
   ___Yes ___ No      1      2      3      4      5
2. The security officer asked if the recipient of the parcel had been contacted to determine if a package was expected.
   ___Yes ___ No
3. The security officer asked if an attempt had been made to iden- tify and contact the sender (if a return address is present).
   ___Yes ___ No      1      2      3      4      5
4. Security officer isolated the package and notified the console by telephone to request a police response.
   ___Yes ___ No      1      2      3      4      5
5. Security officer made liaison with the police and advised them of the threat indicators and action taken thus far to verify the legit- imacy of the package.
   ___Yes ___ No      1      2      3      4      5
6. Security officer completed incident report (grade quality of report)
   ___Yes ___ No      1      2      3      4      5

## EVALUATOR CHECKLIST: ELEVATOR ENTRAPMENT

Trainee: _____        Date: _____
Evaluator: _____        Time: _____

The evaluator will grade the trainee on each of the following criteria. Indicate yes or no and circle the appropriate number regarding the trainee's response.

1 = Poor, 2 = Fair, 3 = Good, 4 = Very Good, 5 = Excellent

Scenario: The security officer in the lobby receives an elevator alarm. It is determined that three people are trapped inside the elevator car.

1. The security officer established communication with the entrapped people using the elevator intercom (grade on calmness, communication skills).
  ___ Yes ___ No     1     2     3     4     5
2. The security officer asked if everyone was okay.
  ___ Yes ___ No
3. The security officer notified the entrapped people that help would be summoned.
  ___ Yes ___ No
4. Security officer notified elevator service company of entrapment and requested emergency service (grade clarity and completeness).
  ___ Yes ___ No     1     2     3     4     5
5. Security officer notified console operator of situation (grade for clarity and completeness).
  ___ Yes ___ No     1     2     3     4     5
6. Security officer requested names and departments of entrapped occupants.
  ___ Yes ___ No     1     2     3     4     5
7. Security officer notified entrapped personnel that help was forthcoming (grade on communication skills).
  ___ Yes ___ No     1     2     3     4     5
8. Security officer offered to place courtesy calls for elevator occupants (grade on communication skills).
  ___ Yes ___ No     1     2     3     4     5
9. Security officer maintained continuous communication with elevator occupants and reassured them (grade communication skills).
  ___ Yes ___ No
10. Security officer completed incident report (grade on quality of report).
  ___ Yes ___ No     1     2     3     4     5

## EVALUATOR CHECKLIST: CIVIL DISTURBANCE (SUPERVISOR)

Trainee: ___          Date: ___
Evaluator: ___ ___    Time: ___

The evaluator will grade the trainee on each of the following criteria. Indicate yes or no and circle the appropriate number regarding the trainee's response.

1 = Poor, 2 = Fair, 3 = Good, 4 = Very Good, 5 = Excellent

Scenario: The security supervisor is notified that a large group of demonstrators (50–100) has formed outside the main entrance of the building to protest the company's position on a controversial subject. There was no notification of this protest and no preparations have been made.

1. The security supervisor notified the security director or security manager.
   ___ Yes ___ No
2. The security supervisor directed nonessential entrances to be closed (grade on clarity and completeness of instructions).
   ___ Yes ___ No          1     2     3     4     5
3. The security supervisor redeployed security force members to the vicinity of the main entrance (grade on clarity and completeness of instructions).
   ___ Yes ___ No          1     2     3     4     5
4. Security supervisor posted designated personnel to observe the demonstrators and report their activity to the security console (grade clarity and completeness of instructions).
   ___ Yes ___ No          1     2     3     4     5
5. Security supervisor notified personnel on break to remain in radio contact and be accessible to respond if necessary (grade for clarity and completeness of instructions).
   ___ Yes ___ No          1     2     3     4     5
6. Security supervisor directed console operator to notify police.
   ___ Yes ___ No          1     2     3     4     5
7. Security supervisor coordinated with console operator and security manager to notify building employees of the situation and advise them to remain in the building (grade on communication skills).
   ___ Yes ___ No          1     2     3     4     5
8. Security supervisor directed personnel to complete incident reports (grade on quality of reports).
   ___ Yes ___ No          1     2     3     4     5

## EVALUATOR CHECKLIST: DEALING WITH A DISRUPTIVE PERSON

Trainee: _____        Date: _____
Evaluator: _____        Time: _____

The evaluator will grade the trainee on each of the following criteria. Indicate yes or no and circle the appropriate number regarding the trainee's response.

1 = Poor, 2 = Fair, 3 = Good, 4 = Very Good, 5 = Excellent

Scenario: The security officer is directed to report to the reception desk in the main lobby to assist the receptionist in dealing with an unruly visitor. Upon arriving in the lobby the security officer encounters the visitor, who is very upset because the employee that the visitor wants to meet with is refusing to see the visitor without an appointment. The visitor informs the security officer that he will not leave unless the meeting takes place.

1. The security officer politely explained the company policy regarding visitors (grade for communication skills).
   ___ Yes ___ No        1        2        3        4        5
2. The security officer maintained a safe distance from the visitor.
   ___ Yes ___ No
3. The security officer used nonthreatening, communicative body language (grade on body language).
   ___ Yes ___ No        1        2        3        4        5
4. Security officer offered alternative methods to the visitor in a polite way: for example, schedule an appointment (grade on communication skills).
   ___ Yes ___ No        1        2        3        4        5
5. Security officer set clearly defined limits for visitor (grade for communication skills/clarity and completeness of instructions).
   ___ Yes ___ No        1        2        3        4        5
6. Security officer explained that the building is private property and, if necessary, the police would be called (grade on communication skills/clarity and completeness of instructions).
   ___ Yes ___ No        1        2        3        4        5
7. Security officer maintained safe position throughout confrontation (grade on stance/body language).
   ___ Yes ___ No        1        2        3        4        5
8. Security officer completed incident report (grade on quality of report).
   ___ Yes ___ No        1        2        3        4        5

## EVALUATOR CHECKLIST: BOMB SEARCH (SHIFT SUPERVISOR)

Trainee. _____          Date· __ __

Evaluator. ___ __          Time· _____

The evaluator will grade the trainee on each of the following criteria. Indicate yes or no and circle the appropriate number regarding the trainee's response.

1 = Poor, 2 = Fair, 3 = Good, 4 = Very Good, 5 = Excellent

Scenario: A telephone bomb threat has been received. While awaiting the arrival of the police, the security manager directs the shift supervisor to begin a search for any suspicious item that may be a bomb. The caller has provided no information regarding the location of the bomb.

1. The supervisor alerted the security force to terminate radio use.
   ___ Yes ___ No
2. The supervisor assigned search teams.
   ___ Yes ___ No
3. The supervisor designated priority search areas (grade on clarity and completeness of instructions).
   ___ Yes ___ No        1      2      3      4      5
4. Supervisor ensured search teams marked off secure areas as they cleared them.
   ___ Yes ___ No
5. Supervisor monitored search teams (grade on communication skills/clarity and completeness of instructions).
   ___ Yes ___ No        1      2      3      4      5
6. Supervisor designated security officer to meet police and escort them to the security console.
   __ Yes ___ No

# Appendix F
## *Skills Practical Application Checklists*

Appendix F gives some examples of skills checklists that can be used for practical application training and testing. While these checklists cover some of the common security tasks, this format can be used to create checklists for any physical skill or task. Most of the skill checklists included here are fairly elementary. They may be made as simple or complex as the trainer feels is appropriate. The checklists are designed to be pass/fail and do not distinguish between different levels of proficiency as do the scenario checklists.

## PERSONNEL ACCESS CONTROL

While assigned to a post where screening of personnel is required, the trainee will complete the following skills in the presence of an evaluator.

- Visually identify a company identification card when it is presented.
- Visually confirm that the picture on the identification card matches the bearer.
- Distinguish a visitor day pass.
- Confirm the visitor pass is for the proper day and has not expired.
- Distinguish a contractor day pass.
- Confirm the contractor pass is for the proper day and has not expired.
- Distinguish a temporary employee identification card.
- Confirm that the temporary employee identification has not expired.
- Demonstrate the procedures for dealing with an employee with no ID card.
- Demonstrate the procedures for dealing with a visitor with no pass or a nonvalid pass.
- Demonstrate the procedure for dealing with a contractor with no pass or a nonvalid pass.
- Demonstrate the procedure for dealing with a temporary employee with no ID or a nonvalid ID.

Trainee: _____
Evaluator: _____
Date: _____

## VEHICLE ACCESS CONTROL

While assigned to a post requiring the screening of vehicles entering company property, the trainee will perform the following skills in the presence of an evaluator.

- Visually identify a company employee sticker affixed on a vehicle.
- Visually confirm that the sticker is valid.
- Visually identify a temporary parking placard.
- Visually confirm that the placard is valid.
- Demonstrate dealing with a vehicle authorized by memo.
- Demonstrate dealing with a delivery vehicle.
- Demonstrate dealing with an unauthorized vehicle that attempts to enter company property.
- Demonstrate checking seals on a company delivery vehicle.
- Demonstrate the procedure for dealing with a broken seal.

Trainee: _____

Evaluator: _____

Date: _____

## VISITOR RECEPTION

While assigned to the reception area, the trainee will demonstrate the skills for screening and directing visitors in the presence of an evaluator.

- Receive a visitor and gather pertinent information.
- Demonstrate locating and notifying a contact person.
- Demonstrate issuance of a visitor pass.
- Demonstrate recording visitor information.
- Demonstrate directing the visitor to the appropriate destination.
- Demonstrate refusing admittance to a visitor.
- Demonstrate use of panic button/call for assistance.
- Explain method for locating contact people within the company.

Trainee: _____

Evaluator: _____

Date: _____

## PROPERTY REMOVAL

While assigned to a post controlling egress from company property, the trainee will demonstrate the following skills in the presence of an evaluator.

- Explain the various portions of the property pass
- Demonstrate checking an employee removing property.
- Demonstrate ensuring the property being removed matches the property described on the pass.
- If property includes computer equipment, demonstrate ensuring that serial numbers are included on the pass.
- Demonstrate matching serial numbers on equipment to serial numbers on pass.
- Visually inspect the pass for a signature.
- Demonstrate the procedure for matching signature with authorized signatory list.
- Demonstrate dealing with a person attempting to remove property without a pass.
- Demonstrate dealing with a property pass signed by someone other than an authorized signatory.

Trainee: _____

Evaluator: _____

Date: _____

## PERIMETER PATROL

While assigned to the perimeter patrol of the company property, the trainee will perform the following skills in the presence of an evaluator.

- ◆ Demonstrate the entire patrol area to be covered during the perimeter patrol.
- ◆ Demonstrate route and schedule variance in the conduct of the patrol.
- ◆ Demonstrate method for checking fence line for vulnerabilities.
- ◆ Identify possible threats that may be encountered. Display threat awareness.
- ◆ Identify vulnerabilities that may exist in the fence line/perimeter barrier.
- ◆ Demonstrate patrol methods in hours of darkness (if applicable).
- ◆ Demonstrate procedure for requesting assistance in the event of an emergency.

Trainee: _____

Evaluator: _____

Date: _____

## FLOOR PATROL

When assigned to complete a building floor patrol during nonworking hours, the trainee will demonstrate the following skills in the presence of an evaluator.

- ◆ Demonstrate knowledge of patrol route.
- ◆ Demonstrate route and schedule variance in the conduct of the patrol.
- ◆ Demonstrate checking office space for safety/fire hazards.
- ◆ Document employees working in office spaces.
- ◆ Document equipment/valuables left unsecured/unattended.
- ◆ Document equipment left on (copiers, coffee machines, etc.) and correct.
- ◆ Document unsecured doors/offices.
- ◆ Demonstrate stairwell patrol.
- ◆ Document safety/fire/maintenance problems observed.

Trainee: _____

Evaluator: _____

Date: _____

## FIRE ALARM PANEL

When assigned to the fire alarm panel, the trainee will demonstrate response to a fire alarm in the presence of an evaluator.

- Demonstrate appropriate actions upon receiving an alarm at the fire panel.
- Demonstrate use of the public address system to alert employees to alarm condition.
- Demonstrate notification of supervisory/management personnel.
- Demonstrate activation of the fire brigade.
- Demonstrate actions upon arrival of fire department personnel.
- Demonstrate postincident documentation.

Trainee: _____
Evaluator: _____
Date: _____

## PORTABLE RADIO USAGE

The trainee will be provided with a portable radio and will demonstrate the following skills in the presence of an evaluator.

- Demonstrate setting the proper channel.
- Demonstrate requesting and receiving a radio communication check.
- Demonstrate proper knowledge of radio codes.
- Demonstrate proper knowledge of radio etiquette.

Trainee: _____
Evaluator: _____
Date: _____

## INTERNAL TELEPHONE SYSTEM USAGE

When provided with a multiline company telephone, the trainee will demonstrate the following skills in the presence of an evaluator.

+ Demonstrate receiving an incoming telephone call and display proper etiquette.
+ Demonstrate transferring a call to a different extension.
+ Demonstrate receiving several calls and conferencing them.
+ Demonstrate getting an outside extension.

Trainee: _____
Evaluator: _____
Date: _____

## PUBLIC ADDRESS SYSTEM USAGE

When provided with the building public address system, the trainee will demonstrate the following skills in the presence of an evaluator.

+ Demonstrate an "all call" to all floors.
+ Demonstrate a call to selected floors.
+ Describe the use of the P.A. system in the event of a fire.
+ Describe the use of the P.A. system during a building evacuation.

Trainee: _____
Evaluator: _____
Date: _____

## FIRE EXTINGUISHER USAGE

When provided with one $CO_2$ fire extinguisher, the trainee will demonstrate the following skills in the presence of an evaluator.

- Demonstrate pulling the pin to arm the extinguisher.
- Demonstrate aiming the nozzle of the extinguisher at the fire.
- Demonstrate squeezing the handle to discharge the extinguisher.
- Demonstrate using the extinguisher in a sweeping motion across the fire area.
- Demonstrate completely expending the contents of the extinguisher.
- Explain the postincident procedure to have the extinguisher recharged.

Trainee: _____
Evaluator: _____
Date: _____

## CARDIOPULMONARY RESUSCITATION

The trainee will be tested on this only after having completed a recognized certification course conducted under the auspices of the American Red Cross or American Heart Association. The trainee will be presented with a simulated casualty and will demonstrate the following skills in the presence of an evaluator.

- ◆ Demonstrate checking for airway/breathing/circulation.
- ◆ Demonstrate notifying EMS.
- ◆ Demonstrate clearing airway.
- ◆ Demonstrate head tilt.
- ◆ Demonstrate rescue breathing.
- ◆ Demonstrate chest compressions.
- ◆ Demonstrate one-person CPR.
- ◆ Demonstrate two-person CPR (if applicable).

Trainee: _____

Evaluator: _____

Date: _____

## RESPONSE TO CHOKING VICTIM

The trainee will be tested on this only after having completed training conducted under the auspices of a recognized authority. The trainee will be presented with a simulated casualty representing a choking victim and will demonstrate the following skills in the presence of an evaluator.

- ◆ Demonstrate determining if the airway is blocked.
- ◆ Demonstrate the Heimlich maneuver in the standing position.
- ◆ Demonstrate the Heimlich maneuver on a prone victim.

Trainee: _____

Evaluator: _____

Date: _____

## RESPONDING TO SHOCK VICTIM

The trainee will be tested on this only after completing a recognized training course. The trainee will be presented with a simulated casualty representing a victim in shock. The trainee will respond by demonstrating the following skills in the presence of an evaluator.

- Describe symptoms of shock.
- Demonstrate checking airway/breathing/circulation.
- Demonstrate requesting emergency assistance.
- Demonstrate elevating victim's feet.
- Demonstrate loosening victim's clothing.
- Demonstrate covering victim for warmth.
- Demonstrate reassuring victim.

Trainee: _____
Evaluator: _____
Date: _____

## RESPONDING TO SEIZURE VICTIM

The trainee will be tested on this only after completing a recognized training course. The trainee will be presented with a simulated casualty who will represent a seizure victim. The trainee will demonstrate the following skills in the presence of an evaluator.

- Describe the symptoms typical of seizure activity.
- Demonstrate requesting emergency assistance.
- Demonstrate safeguarding the victim during the seizure activity to prevent a serious injury.
- Demonstrate placing the victim on her side following the seizure and awaiting medical response.

Trainee: _____
Evaluator: _____
Date: _____

# RESPONDING TO A VICTIM WITH DEEP LACERATIONS/BLEEDING

The trainee will be tested on this only after completing a recognized training course. The trainee will be presented with a simulated casualty representing a person with deep lacerations/profuse bleeding. The trainee may be provided with a first aid kit including pressure bandages and latex gloves or may be asked to improvise from the environment. The trainee will demonstrate the following skills in the presence of an evaluator.

+ Demonstrate requesting immediate medical assistance.
+ Demonstrate applying pressure to the wound to stop the bleeding.
+ Demonstrate treatment for shock.
+ Demonstrate use of protective barrier equipment (i.e., latex gloves).

Trainee: _____
Evaluator: _____
Date: _____

## 9 mm SEMIAUTOMATIC PISTOL
## MAINTENANCE AND INSPECTION

This testing will be strictly for security personnel armed with the 9 mm semiautomatic pistol. These personnel will have completed a safety course, basic qualification course, and tactical firing course conducted by an approved authority. The trainee will be provided with one 9 mm semiautomatic pistol, one cleaning kit, ten rounds of training ammunition, and one empty magazine. The trainee will demonstrate the following skills in the presence of an evaluator.

- Clear weapon and inspect for safety purposes.
- Disassemble weapon.
- Reassemble weapon.
- Demonstrate procedures for cleaning weapon.
- Demonstrate loading magazine using training ammunition.
- Demonstrate loading weapon.
- Demonstrate chambering a round using training ammunition.
- Demonstrate clearing weapon using training ammunition.
- Demonstrate unloading magazine using training ammunition.
- Display "complete safe" weapon.

Trainee: _____

Evaluator: _____

Date: _____

# Appendix G
## *Sample Practical Training Schedule*

Appendix G describes an example of a practical training cycle from beginning to end. There is a class outline, a class handout that covers all the material to be covered in the class, a written examination, and a round-robin practical exercise schedule.

### TERRORISM THREAT AWARENESS AND BOMB THREAT/SUSPECT ITEM INCIDENT RESPONSE

   I. Introduction
   1. Purpose of this training.
   2. Overview.
   II. Terrorism Awareness
   1. Recent events.
   2. Relevance to security officers.
   3. Threat assessment.
   4. Definitions of terrorism.
   5. International vs. domestic terrorism.
   6. Characteristics, goals, and organization of terrorist groups.

    7. Terrorist methods, tactics, and sequence of actions.
    8. Pre-incident phase: recognizing terrorist intelligence
       techniques.
    9. Examples of terrorist incidents in the United States.
  III. Bomb Threat/Suspect Item Response
    1. Bomb/IED as terrorist weapon of choice.
    2. Classifications of bombs/IEDs.
    3. Frequency of incidents in United States.
    4. Overview of three principle classifications of incidents.
    5. Telephone bomb threat response.
    6. Bomb search in response to a bomb threat.
    7. Response to suspect item discovered on premises.
    8. Suspect postal item: characteristics and response.
  IV. Written Examination
   V. Meal Break
  VI. Facility Walk-Through
 VII. Practical Training Round-Robin

## Introduction

The purpose of this training is to make the security staff more aware of the threat of terrorism and to reacquaint the security officers with techniques regarding the proper response to possible bomb incidents. While all security officers have received training on bomb threats and bomb incidents, there may be a gap between understanding the skills and recognizing the reality of the threat. This class will address that gap.

    The class will consist of two sections. The first section will familiarize the security officer with terrorism in general with an emphasis on recognizing terrorist methods and tactics. The second section will discuss procedures developed by the security department for responding to these situations.

## Terrorism Awareness

It is important for security officers to recognize that this threat exists to a greater or lesser extent at all times. Special alerts may take place in response to world warning, but security officers must be vigilant at all times to this danger.

If a corporation is based in the downtown business district of a large city, there are numerous reasons why it is an attractive target:

1. The business district is known as a center of international finance and is a symbol of capitalism despised by many extremist groups.
2. It is in close proximity to other large corporations.
3. It is in close proximity to several major transportation hubs, which are attractive targets.
4. It is not far from government buildings which may be the target of various groups.
5. Due to the relatively high security at the aforementioned locations, the company headquarters may be considered a "soft target."
6. Due to the controversial nature of some of the company's global business policies, it may be the target of extremist groups.

**Definitions of Terrorism**

There are numerous definitions of terrorism used by different agencies. One of the most concise is "the calculated use of violence to attain political goals through the use of intimidation and fear."

**International versus Domestic Terrorism**

International terrorist groups have originated abroad; however, they may have developed a base in and conduct operations in the United States. Some examples are:

1. Hamas
2. Hezbollah
3. Islamic Jihad
4. Abu Nidal Organization
5. Jama Islamiya

Domestic terrorist groups have originated in the United States and include not only political groups but also radical environmental, animal rights, and anti-abortion groups. Some examples are:

1. FALN
2. Aryan Nations
3. Army of God
4. Christian Identity Movement

## Characteristics of Terrorist Groups

1. Seek to promote fear.
2. Can function relatively effectively with limited resources/manpower.
3. Are usually very mobile.
4. Use small groups/cell structure for efficiency and security.
5. May be willing to die to accomplish their mission.

## Terrorist Goals

Goals vary depending on the group. There is a trend now for groups to strike without claiming responsibility. Some possible goals include:

1. Obtain worldwide recognition (when responsibility *is* claimed).
2. Weaken or embarrass target government.
3. Show a government's inability to protect its citizens.
4. Demonstrate power or threat credibility.

## Terrorist Organization

|  | COMMAND ELEMENT |  |
| --- | --- | --- |
| INTELLIGENCE SECTION | SUPPORT SECTION | TACTICAL UNITS |

(Each Unit has 2–3 cells of 2–5 persons each)

### Terrorist Methods

1. Bombing (most prevalent)
2. Arson
3. Assassination
4. Kidnapping
5. Hijacking
6. Hostage taking

## Terrorist Tactics

1. Operate clandestinely.
2. Use cell structure for security purposes.
3. Merge with local people.
4. Make use of fake ID, cover stories.
5. Conduct preassault reconnaissance of target.
6. May be willing to sacrifice themselves to accomplish mission.

## Sequence of Actions

I. Preincident Phase
 1. Extensive target reconnaissance
 2. Development of plan
 3. Designation of alternate targets
II. Initiation Phase
 1. Movement to target area
III. Negotiation Phase (not present in all incidents): applies primarily to hostage taking, kidnapping, and hijacking incidents
IV. Climax Phase
 1. Often immediately follows the Initiation Phase
 2. Involves the action itself
V. Postincident Phase
 1. Withdrawal from the target area
 2. Regroup and critique incident

**Pre-Incident Phase:**  Recognizing Terrorist Intelligence Gathering Techniques

This is probably the most important phase for the security officer to recognize. It is not practical to assume that the security officer will necessarily be able to prevent the incident once it has reached the initiation or climax phases. Detection, deterrence, and reporting by the security officer will be the key at this phase. Through detection, the security officer will ideally identify the terrorist reconnaissance or will identify a suspicious item in the case of the initiation phase. By establishing a visible presence, the security officer will deter the terrorists during the reconnaissance and encourage them to seek a less secure target. Through reporting, the security officer will make company management and law enforcement authorities aware of the threat.

There are four sources the terrorist group can use to gather intelligence about a target:

1. Human Intelligence (HUMINT), gathered by people in the area.
2. Signals Intelligence (SIGINT), the interception of communication signals
3. Photo Intelligence (PHOTINT), photographing the site
4. Operational Patterns, observing patterns of activity at site

By recognizing these methods of intelligence gathering, we can take action to reduce the threat of an attack. Some characteristics to be aware of include:

1. People loitering around the building, or taking an unusual interest in the building or activities at the building.
2. People photographing or sketching the building.
3. People asking questions about security or security procedures at the building.
4. People attempting to gain access into the building.

The following are some steps that can be taken to further reduce the likelihood that the building will be chosen as a target:

1. Do not give any information about the building or building procedures to strangers.
2. Report any contact with people asking inappropriate questions or loitering around the facility to security department management.
3. Challenge anyone who may be unauthorized or anyone who appears unfamiliar with the building. Be tactful, but firmly ask, "May I help you?"
4. Vary patrol times and routes when doing the exterior patrol.
5. Be vigilant both on patrol and at a fixed post.

### Recent Examples of Terrorism in the United States

- 1993 bombing of the World Trade Center in New York City
- 1995 bombing of the Alfred P. Murrah Federal Building in Oklahoma City
- 1996 bombing at Centennial Olympic Park in Atlanta
- 1997 bombing at an abortion clinic in Atlanta
- 1997 bombing at a nightclub in Atlanta

These incidents represent only some of the more dramatic and widely reported occurrences. By studying these incidents and a broad range of terrorist actions that have occurred abroad, we can detect several trends that are becoming common in terrorist activity:

1. No bomb threat or warning phone call.
2. Vehicles used to carry more explosives/make bomb more powerful.
3. Vehicle can be very destructive even parked outside the facility.
4. Secondary device may be present.

### Bomb Threat/Suspect Item Response

The improvised bomb, also referred to as an improvised explosive device (IED) is the weapon of choice for terrorists as well as many other disaffected people (such as the Unabomber). Bombs/IEDs can be classified numerous ways, including by type of explosive used (high or low) or by firing system (electrical or nonelectrical). Bombs can also be classified by delivery and activation methods:

## Delivery Methods
◆ Vehicle
◆ Laid (placed by hand)
◆ Projectile (thrown or launched)
◆ Postal

## Activation Methods
◆ Command detonation
◆ Action by target (i.e., booby-trap)
◆ Time delay

### *Three Principle Classifications of Incidents*

The following are the three principle types of bomb incidents we are likely to encounter. Each type of incident will be discussed with the appropriate response.

I. Telephone Bomb Threat (attachment: FBI bomb threat checklist)
   1. Two possible motives for bomb threat
   2. Response procedures
   3. Search procedures (attachment: Bureau of Alcohol, Tobacco and Firearms bulletin on search procedures)
II. Suspect Item Discovered on Premises
   1. Isolation procedures
   2. Notification procedures
III. Postal/Letter/Parcel Bomb
   1. Identifying characteristics (attachment: U.S. Postal Inspection Service bulletin on mail bomb characteristics)
   2. Isolation procedures
   3. Notification procedures

When encountering a bomb threat or suspect item, take the following actions:

1. Notify the police immediately as well as company security department management
2. DO NOT touch or move the item!
3. Beware of antihandling devices on the item
4. Beware of secondary devices.
5. Do not use radios in the presence of a suspect item or during a search unless directed to do so by the police.

### Written Examination on Terrorism Awareness and Bomb Threat/Suspect Item Reponse

1. The threat considerations at the company headquarters consist of all the following *except*:
   a. Its location in the business district.
   b. The business of the company.
   c. The close proximity to agricultural areas.
   d. The close proximity to the major businesses.
2. Name three examples of international terrorist groups.
   _____
   _____
   _____
3. Name three examples of domestic terrorist groups.
   _____
   _____
   _____
4. What are the four elements usually found in a terrorist organization?
   _____
   _____
   _____
   _____
5. Which element gathers information on the target?
   _____
6. Which element gathers equipment and arranges transportation and lodging?
   _____

7. Which element carries out the actual attack?

   _____

8. What characterizes the preincident phase?

   _____

9. At what stage can the security officer best deter the terrorists and why?

   _____

10. What are the four sources of intelligence for terrorist groups?

    _____

    _____

    _____

    _____

11. Which source of intelligence is characterized by engaging people in conversation?

    _____

12. Name two characteristics of intelligence gathering you may see that could indicate a problem.

    _____

    _____

13. Name two incidents mentioned in the case studies where a second device was used.

    _____

    _____

14. Name the four possible delivery methods for an IED.

    _____

    _____

    _____

    _____

15. Name three activation methods for IEDs.

    _____

    _____

    _____

16. What are two possible motives for a bomb threat phone call?

    _____

    _____

17. Generally, by how many feet should a suspect item be isolated?
    1. 10 feet
    2. 100–300 feet
    3. 300–1,000 feet
    4. 20–30 feet
18. Where can procedures for dealing with a bomb incident at the company headquarters be found?

    _____

19. Who should be notified in the event of a suspicious item or telephone bomb threat?

    _____

20. What can be used to mark off the area where a suspect item is located?

    _____

### Facility Walk-Through

The instructor will lead the trainees through the facility to give them a greater appreciation of priority search areas, standoff distances, evacuation rally points, and so on.

### Practical Training Round-Robin

Following the completion of the written examination, the trainees will be divided into four groups of four persons each. Each group will be assigned to a training station. Each training station will specialize in a particular practical skill and will be administered by an evaluator. Trainees will spend one hour at each station before rotating to the next station. The groups will be numbered one through four. Group One will begin at Station One, Group Two at Station Two, and so on. When rotating, the group will move to the next numerical station. The evaluator at each station will evaluate the trainees and record their responses on a checklist.

- Station One: Receiving a Bomb Threat Phone Call. At this station trainees will listen to simulated threat phone calls and will be graded on their ability to recognize and record information, ask questions, and take appropriate post-threat call notification and response measures.

♦ Station Two: Conducting a Search Following Receipt of a Bomb Threat Call. At this station trainees will simulate conducting a search using proper search techniques, and if a suspect item is found will take appropriate action to isolate it and make notification.

♦ Station Three: Varied Suspect Item Scenarios. At this station, the trainees will be confronted with various scenarios involving a suspect item being discovered or reported by an employee, but no threat call received. Scenarios involving suspect vehicles will also be utilized. The trainees will be evaluated on their ability to apply the lessons taught in the classroom to these situations.

♦ Station Four: Suspect Parcel/Envelope Response. Trainees at this station will be given an opportunity to manually screen envelopes and parcels and identify those which may constitute a possible threat. Trainees will be evaluated on their ability to recognize indicators taught in the classroom portion, their attempts to verify the item, and when necessary, isolation of the suspect item.

# Appendix H
## *Immediate Action Drills*

As noted in Chapter Six, immediate action drills can be used to train set responses to relatively uncomplicated situations. Immediate action drills must be kept simple and practiced frequently to be truly effective.

## FIRE ALARM

Situation: A fire alarm is received on the fire panel.
    Response:

1. Acknowledge alarm and identify affected area. Make P.A. announcement to building occupants notifying them that an alarm has been received, is being investigated, and that further information will be forthcoming. Maintain communication with building occupants, updating them on situation. Coordinate evacuation of affected areas, if necessary.
2. Notify fire department as back-up for central station automatic notification. Place call to security management and facility management representatives to notify them of the situation.

3. Assume position at main entrance to make liaison with fire department personnel. Bring company fire plan (to include floor plans).

## INTRUDER BREACHING ACCESS CONTROL POINT

Situation: An individual breaches or bypasses the access control point and attempts to enter the core of the building.
  Response:

1. Automatically recall and shut down all the elevators to prevent the individual from getting to any of the floors.
2. Approach the individual and, while maintaining a safe distance, challenge the person for identification.
3. Notify the police and security management and request immediate assistance.
4. Prepare to make liaison with the police upon their arrival and escort them to the incident scene.

## SUSPICIOUS ITEM ON PREMISES

Situation: An employee has reported an unattended bag left in the building.
  Response:

1. Respond to area where item was seen and isolate the immediate area. Remain outside isolated area to prevent people from entering it.
2. Notify police and security management.
3. Assume post at main entrance to make liaison with police and lead them to the suspect item.

## HAZARDOUS MATERIALS INCIDENT

Situation: Members of the cleaning staff alert security that a powerful chemical cleaner is leaking rapidly from its storage container.

Response:

1. Isolate the area where the substance is located. Remain posted in a safe area outside the isolated area to direct people away from the isolated area.
2. Notify the fire department, security management, and facilities/engineering management of the incident.
3. Locate the respective material safety data sheet for that substance. Await arrival of the fire department HAZMAT unit to make liaison and guide to the affected area.

## MEDICAL EMERGENCY

Situation: Security receives a call that there is a sick/injured person in need of immediate medical attention.

Response:

1. Respond to the area where the sick/injured person is located. Perform first-aid only if absolutely necessary. Gather information from victim and witnesses.
2. Call for an ambulance. Notify security management about the incident.
3. Place elevator on standby for the paramedics. Prepare to operate elevator.
4. Wait for paramedics' arrival. Serve as escort for paramedics throughout the situation. Gather pertinent information such as paramedics' IDs, hospital the victim will be taken to, and so on.

## ELEVATOR ENTRAPMENT

Situation: Security receives an elevator alarm. Upon making contact with the elevator occupants by intercom, it is learned that the elevator is stuck with several people inside.

Response:

1. Remain in constant communication with the entrapped occupants by intercom. Reassure the occupants that help is on the way. Learn the identity of the occupants and offer to make courtesy phone calls to anyone they may need contacted.
2. Notify the elevator service company. Request a mechanic be dispatched immediately. Notify security management and facilities/engineering management.

# Index

LaVergne, TN USA
18 November 2009
164471LV00005B/4/A

9 780750 671590